CISTERCIAN STUDIES SERIES: NUMBER TWO HUNDRED NINETY

Premonstratensian Texts and Studies, 3

Jacob Panhausen

Two Sixteenth-Century Premonstratensian Treatises on Religious Life

Translated and Introduced by William P. Hyland

α

Cistercian Publications
www.cistercianpublications.org

LITURGICAL PRESS
Collegeville, Minnesota
www.litpress.org

A Cistercian Publications title published by Liturgical Press

Cistercian Publications
Editorial Offices
161 Grosvenor Street
Athens, Ohio 45701
www.cistercianpublications.org

Biblical citations are based on *The Holy Bible: Douay Rheims Version* (Baltimore: John Murphy, 1899; repr. Rockford, Illinois: Tan, 1971), with minimal modernization. All rights reserved.

1   2   3   4   5   6   7   8   9

Library of Congress Cataloging-in-Publication Data

Names: Panhausen, Jacob, author. | Hyland, William P., translator. | Panhausen, Jacob. Ad praelatos et subditos pia exhortatio. English. | Panhausen, Jacob. Tractatus de monasticae vitae cultoribus atque religiosorum votis etc. English.

Title: Two sixteenth-century Premonstratensian treatises on religious life / Jacob Panhausen ; translated and introduced by William P. Hyland.

Description: Collegeville, Minnesota : Cistercian Publications/Liturgical Press, [2021] | Series: Cistercian studies series ; number two hundred ninety | Includes bibliographical references. | Summary: "This volume presents a translation, for the first time in English, of two Latin texts by Jacob Panhausen, A Loving Exhortation to Prelates and Those in Their Charge and Treatise on Monastic Life and Religious Vows. The introduction offers a biographical and analytical overview of this Norbertine reformer, illuminating a crucial time in the renewal of the Premonstratensian Order during and after the Council of Trent"— Provided by publisher.

Identifiers: LCCN 2020041279 (print) | LCCN 2020041280 (ebook) | ISBN 9780879072902 (paperback) | ISBN 9780879075903 (epub) | ISBN 9780879075903 (mobi) | ISBN 9780879075903 (pdf)

Subjects: LCSH: Premonstratensians—Spiritual life. | Premonstratensians—History—Sources.

Classification: LCC BX3903 .P36 2021 (print) | LCC BX3903 (ebook) | DDC 255/.19—dc23

LC record available at https://lccn.loc.gov/2020041279

LC ebook record available at https://lccn.loc.gov/2020041280

"Reformation scholars owe William Hyland a considerable debt for his fine edition and translation of two of Abbot Jacob Panhausen's treatises on the religious life. Written at a time of great upheaval, Panhausen's texts reveal his deep roots in medieval monastic spirituality and devotion as well as his connections to new Christocentric currents of humanist reform. As Hyland's excellent introduction suggests they thus provide a rare and invaluable view into the theology and devotion of a leading reforming Abbot and Catholic irenic, serving as a reminder of a rich stream of monastic reform which continued even amid the struggles of Reformers and Counter-Reformers alike. Abbot Panhausen deserves to be widely read, and Hyland's volume is the perfect companion for anyone venturing into his world and that of sixteenth-century Premonstratensian reform more generally."

—Simon J. G. Burton
John Laing Senior Lecturer in Reformation History
School of Divinity, University of Edinburgh

"We are indebted to William P. Hyland for his translation of two texts that illuminate how a reform-minded abbot grounded in church traditions and embracing humanism was able to navigate a path to renewal during distressing times. Hyland's introduction and translations demonstrate how, in the crucible of early modernity, the moderate reformer Jacob Panhausen tried to find a bridge between Catholics and Protestants—defending his heritage while embracing criticisms and calls for renewal."

—Christopher M. Bellitto
Professor of History
Kean University

To my beloved wife Sabine

Contents

Acknowledgments

This project grew out of a deep interest in the Premonstratensians in the later Middle Ages. For this I must ultimately thank my *Doktorvater* James J. John, who inspired a love of Premonstratensian history and palaeography, and taught me to seek out new texts and take the exciting and sometimes daunting step to study figures whose significance and importance has not previously been appreciated. Concerning the current volume, I have built upon the work of Bernard Ardura, which first drew my attention to Jacob Panhausen, and of Jean-Baptiste Valvekens, who made Panhausen's texts accessible.

The project has extended over several years, delayed at points by various illnesses, and also by moving across the ocean. I am indebted to the assistance of the library staffs at St. Norbert College and the University of St. Andrews, and to supportive colleagues at those institutions. At St. Norbert, I would like to thank Rosemary Sands, the Director of the Center for Norbertine Studies, for all of her indispensable help in bringing this volume to fruition, and to Julie Massey for her support. Wolfgang Grassl, who shares my interest in probing into the corners of Premonstratensian history, also offered kind support and encouragement in the earliest stages of this project. Parts of this research have been discussed in various research seminars in the School of Divinity at the University of St. Andrews, and I am thankful for the support and insights of my colleagues. Mark Elliott in particular kindly read a draft of this work and gave his usual insightful advice.

Carol Neel has been incredibly helpful at every stage of this work, from its conception through the final stages. Her keen editorial skills and unparalleled knowledge of Norbertine spirituality, along with her friendship, good humor, and constant support, cannot be acknowledged enough. I am also very grateful to Marsha Dutton of Cistercian Publications for her editorial acumen, advice, patience, and kind empathy in the final stages of this project, and for the support of Hans Christofferson and the design team at Liturgical Press.

The opportunity to work in tandem with Premonstratensian canons as friends and colleagues is something for which I am eminently grateful. I would like in particular to mention Fr. Hermann Janssens of Averbode Abbey for providing me with a digital copy of the Averbode manuscript of Abbot Panhausen's writings. I have benefited from the encouragement of Norbertine Fathers Hugh Barbour, Andrew Ciferni, Ambrose Criste, and Theodore Antry. For his friendship and support I feel a particular debt of gratitude to Fr. Antry, who passed away while this book was in its final stages of production. The generous financial support of the Norbertine abbeys of De Pere, Albuquerque, Daylesford, and Orange, along with St. Norbert College and the Definitory of the Premonstratensian Order, made this volume possible and continues their essential support of the Premonstratensian Texts and Studies series.

The unwavering support of my daughters Margaret and Eleanor has been a constant source of comfort. I would be remiss to omit mention of my faithful feline contemplative companions Poe and Loki. To my wife Sabine, to whom this book is dedicated, for her scholarly insights, wisdom, never-failing faith, and encouragement, I owe more than I can even begin to adequately express.

William P. Hyland
School of Divinity
University of St. Andrews

Introduction

The Premonstratensians in the Sixteenth Century

In a time of internal institutional decline and external challenges, what is the possible remedy for a renewal of religious life? How can one be faithful to a centuries-old way of life while at the same time responsive to the needs and demands of contemporary society? How can an older religious order remain faithful to its charism while at the same time answering the challenges of totally new situations, including the challenge of Protestantism? The Premonstratensian Order, burdened by the problems facing many older orders by the sixteenth century, would find the inspiration to rise to these challenges through a rejuvenated commitment to its distinctive way of life—rooted in the ancient teachings of *The Rule of Saint Augustine* and the strong pastoral ideals of the Gregorian reform epitomized by its founder Saint Norbert of Xanten.

An important and often overlooked figure in this crucial time of survival and renewal was Jacob Panhausen, abbot of Steinfeld and vicar general of the Westphalian circary from 1540–1582, a reign begun before the Council of Trent and ending with symbolic force in the same year as the canonization of Saint Norbert. As Bernard Ardura, the prominent historian of the Premonstratensians in the Reformation era, says of Panhausen, "Amid controversies and relaxation on the part of some religious communities, Abbot James Panhausen appears as a zealous prelate and a precursor of regular reform. In that capacity, he deserves to be better known."[1] In the midst of the confessional fault lines in sixteenth-century Germany, where the religious way of life was radically under siege and extremely precarious, the work of Abbot Panhausen stands as a crucial link between the late medieval reformers and the generation after the Council of Trent. His steadfast efforts for renewal helped prepare the way for a "silver age" of the Premonstratensian Order as it endured and even flourished until the French Revolution.

The middle decades of the sixteenth century were not a good time for the Premonstratensian Order. Earlier, at the time of the promulgation of new statutes at the general chapter of 1505, few canons could have foreseen the storm clouds on the horizon.[2] The need for reform had long been acknowledged, and from the fifteenth century onwards sporadic reformist efforts had appeared in some sectors of the Order. Isolated examples of success, such as the well-documented visitation of the English abbeys by Bishop Redman, abbot of Shap and bishop of Ely, or the continuing attempts of the abbots of Steinfeld to coordinate reform in their region of Germany, are documented.[3]

But these efforts did not effectively ameliorate a much larger picture of serious and endemic problems in other parts of the Order. Many of the most important French abbeys, including Prémontré itself, had fallen into *commendam*, a debilitating situation in which the king appointed a prelate

---

1. Bernard Ardura, *The Order of Prémontré: History and Spirituality*, trans. Edward Hagman (De Pere, WI: Paisa Publishing, 1995), 201.

2. See J. B. Valvekens, "Le Chapitre général et les Statuts prémontrés de 1505," *Analecta Praemonstratensia* 13 (1938): 546.

3. On Redman's visitations, see Joseph Gribbin, *The Premonstratensian Order in Late Medieval Britain* (Woodridge: Boydell Press, 2001), 20–100. For Steinfeld's role in reform activities, see Johannes Meier, "Die nordwestdeutschen Pramonstratenser angesichts von Verfall und Reform des Ordens 1350–1550," *Analecta Praemonstratensia* 79 (2003): 25–56.

or layman as abbot, often to the financial and spiritual detriment of an abbey. Difficulties brought on by wars and incipient national rivalries, for instance between France and Spain, deeply imperiled efforts to maintain the central governance of the Order—or any coherent structure at all.[4] The abbeys in Bohemia and Moravia continued to reel from the disruption and physical destruction of the Hussite wars of the fifteenth century, while the promising reform work of Provost Fegyverneky of Saag in Hungary was halted by the Turkish conquest of that kingdom following the Battle of Mohács in 1526.[5] But above all, the rise and spread of Protestantism threatened the elimination of all religious orders, including the Premonstratensians, in those parts of Europe where it proved triumphant. Thus by the middle of the sixteenth century the Norbertine Order had completely disappeared in much of northern and central Germany, Scandinavia, and England, with further losses on the horizon in Scotland, Ireland, and parts of the Low Countries.

The response of individual Premonstratensians to the Protestant movement varied, reflecting the diverse and complex forces at work in the Reformation. Some Norbertines joined the Reformation, and a few well-known Protestant reformers were either themselves Premonstratensians or had very close ties to Premonstratensian circles. Menno Simons, the prominent early Anabaptist leader, was associated with the abbey of Witmarsum in Frisia, and it is likely that early in his career he was a Premonstratensian.[6] Johannes Bugenhagen, who

---

4. For an excellent overview of this period, with bibliography, see Ardura, *The Order of Prémontré*, 147–232.

5. A. Oszvald, "Fegyverneky Ferenc, sági prépsot, rendi visitator. 1506–1535," in *Emlékkönyu Szent Norbert halálának 800 éves jubileumára* (Gödöll: Jászó-Premontrei Kanonkren, 1934), 51–108; see also Ardura, *The Order of Prémontré*, 229–33.

6. See George K. Epp, "The Spiritual Roots of Menno Simons," in *Mennonite Images*, ed. Harry Loewen (Winnipeg: Hyperion Press, 1980), 51–59.

eventually became Martin Luther's personal chaplain in Wittenberg and even officiated at Luther's wedding, is another example. Bugenhagen went on to play an important role in the organization of the Lutheran Church in areas of northern Germany and Scandinavia.[7] Although it is unclear whether he had ever professed as a Premonstratensian canon, he was rector of the Marienkirche school of the Premonstratensian abbey at Treptow in Pomerania, and he also taught in the cloister school at Belbuck abbey.

Abbot Johann Boldewan of Belbuck was also a great supporter of humanistic and Lutheran ideas, and after being deposed by the Edict of Worms in 1522 for heresy, he followed Bugenhagen to Wittenberg and worked for ten years as a Lutheran pastor until his death.[8] Belbuck was perhaps the most influential center of humanism in the Baltic area in the first two decades of the sixteenth century, and after Bugenhagen's departure for Wittenberg in 1521, his successor as rector, Andreas Knopken, soon made it the center for preaching the new Lutheran doctrines.[9] Bugenhagen himself had first been exposed to Lutheran teaching when he was given a copy of Luther's *On the Babylonian Captivity of the Church* by a Premonstratensian of Treptow.[10]

Thus while a few Premonstratensians avidly embraced the new Protestant movement in its various forms, most

---

7. For a recent study of the earlier career of Bugenhagen, see Hans-Günter Leder, *Johannes Bugenhagen Pomeranus—vom Reformer zum Reformator. Studien zur Biographie* (Frankfurt-am-Main: Peter Lang, 2002).

8. See Ferdinand Ahuis, "Johannes Boldewan," in *Auf den zweiten Blick. Frauen und Männer der Nordkirche vom Mittelalter bis zur Gegenwart, Schriften des Vereins für Schleswig-Holsteinische Kirchengeschichte 61;* ed. Claudia Tietz, Ruth Albrecht, and Rainer Hering (Husum: Mathiesen, 2018), 61–69.

9. David Kirby, *Northern Europe in the Early Modern Period: The Baltic World 1492–1772* (London & New York: Longman, 1990), 83–84.

10. Karl August T. Vogt, *Johannes Bugenhagen Pomeranus: Leben und ausgewählte Schriften* (Elberfeldt: R. L. Friderichs, 1867), 29–30.

were displaced from their secularized abbeys and in various ways accommodated themselves to the new reality, either by remaining to minister—now ostensibly as Protestant clergymen—to their flocks in their parish churches, or by retiring and living in seclusion from public life or in exile. As was the case with members of many of the religious orders, some Premonstratensians resisted secularization to the point of martyrdom. A famous example is the English abbot Matthew Mackeral of Barlings, titular bishop of Chalcedon, who was executed by the government for his participation in the failed "Bigod's Rebellion" related to the Pilgrimage of Grace in 1537.[11] And finally, the violence endemic to the sixteenth-century religious conflicts resulted in episodes like the tragedy in 1572 of the Nineteen Martyrs of Gorkum, in the Netherlands, who included the Premonstratensians James Lacobs and Adrian van Hilvaranbeek.[12]

The Protestant Reformation of the sixteenth century moreover challenged and imperiled the very existence of the monastic ideal. This threat, along with longstanding problems such as moral laxity and the widespread persistence of commendatory abbots, urgently required a fresh articulation of the traditional ideals of religious life. This imperative was complemented by a strong humanist impulse among Catholic reformers to look to the early church, particularly the Scriptures and the Fathers, for inspiration and direction. For its part, the Council of Trent in 1563 directed the older religious orders to seek guidance in their

---

11. David Knowles, *Bare Ruined Choirs: The Dissolution of the English Monasteries* (Cambridge: Cambridge University Press, 1976), 217–18. For an overview of the whole subject, see Madeleine Hope Dodds and Ruth Dodds, *The Pilgrimage of Grace 1536–1537 and the Exeter Conspiracy 1538* (Cambridge: Cambridge University Press, 1971).

12. Ardura, *The Order of Prémontré*, 189–92; I. van Spilbeeck, *S. Adrien et S. Jacques, de l'Ordre de Prémontré: Martyrs de Gorcum. Notices historiques* (Brussels-Tamine: Bibliothèque Norbertine, 1900).

renewal by turning to the observance and spirit of their respective rules and ancient discipline.[13] In the case of the Premonstratensians, this meant a renewed attention to the *Rule of Saint Augustine* and the life and work of the founder Norbert of Xanten.[14]

In this grave situation, with the very existence of the order at stake, Nicholas Psaume, first abbot and then bishop of Verdun, began the process of essentially saving the Order and guiding it toward what would eventually become a significant era of reform, revival, and renewal in the seventeenth century. He was followed in this work by another vigorous abbot general, John Despruets. Psaume began the work of articulating a specific spirituality based upon observance of the Augustinian Rule in his capitular orations.[15] Despruets, along with his tireless efforts to knit the Order together on an administrative level and obtain the official canonization of Saint Norbert, produced many writings defending and articulating the spirituality of the order.[16]

The Life and Career of Abbot Jacob Panhausen

In this wide historical context Jacob Panhausen guided his community at Steinfeld through his abbey's and order's crisis.[17] The future abbot was born around 1500 near Liège

---

13. Council of Trent, Session 25, Decree on Reform of Regulars, chap. 1 (1563). For the text, see *Decrees of the Ecumenical Councils*, ed. Norman Tanner (London: Sheed & Ward; Washington, DC: Georgetown University Press, 1990), 2:776.

14. Ardura, *The Order of Prémontré*, 277–80.

15. Bernard Ardura, "Les exhortations capitulaires de Nicolas Psaume," *Analecta Praemonstratensia* 53 (1987): 26–69.

16. Ardura, *The Order of Prémontré*, 235.

17. The following overview of Panhausen's life is drawn from the most detailed biographical treatments to date: André Léon Goovaerts, *Ecrivains, Artistes et Savants de l'Ordre de Prémontré*, 2 vols. (Brussels: Schepens, 1902–

of an important local family and educated there by the Brethren of the Common Life; he completed his studies in Cologne. The school run by the Brethren in Liège had been founded in about 1500 and subsequently enjoyed a fine reputation.[18] The Brethren often employed school teachers from outside their community, although they took direct care of the religious instruction of the students. Thus Panhausen would have absorbed the piety of the Modern Devotion from the Brethren in their pastoral role.

The curriculum as it existed in Liège was later described by the educator John Sturm, who had been a student there from 1521 to 1524. Sturm mentions that, in the humanist spirit, Greek, rhetoric, and law had been added to the earlier curriculum.[19] It is thus likely that the young Panhausen may have learned some Greek, and while there is some anecdotal evidence of his familiarity with the language,[20] there is no clear evidence of extensive knowledge in the writings he produced as an elderly abbot.

Of relevance for Panhausen's education, however, is a letter written by Goswin of Halen to Albert Hardenberg in 1529. Goswin had studied at a school of the Brethren in Deventer, and in his subsequent life as a member of the Brethren's house in Groningen remained acquainted with many leading Dutch humanists, including Erasmus himself.

1907), 2:11–13; Ardura, *The Order of Prémontré*, 198–201, follows J. B. Valvekens, "Jacobus Panhausen, Abbas Steinfeldensis," *Analecta Praemonstratensia* 54 (1978): 99–104. For a useful survey with excellent bibliography, see Jan Gerits, "Jacob Panhuysen van Opoeteren, abt van Steinfeld: Een kloosterhervormer, ascetisch schrijver en humanist uit de 16de eeuw," in *Heemkunde Limburg* 2 (2006): 10–15.

18. R. R. Post discusses the educational activities of the Brethren in this period in *The Modern Devotion: Confrontation with Reformation and Humanism* (Leiden: E. J. Brill, 1968), 551–631, with special reference to Liège, 556–68.

19. Post, *The Modern Devotion*, 558–59.

20. Gerits, "Jacob Panhuysen," 13.

In a letter of 1529, Goswin mentions the following classical authors his friend ought to read: Virgil, Horace, Terence, Plutarch, Sallust, Aristotle, Thucydides, Herodotus, Plato, and Aristotle. Additionally, Goswin recommends Josephus, the Church Fathers, Bernard of Clairvaux, and Hugh of Saint Victor.[21] The fact that many of the same classical and medieval writers are cited by Panhausen, whether directly or through the writings of others, points to his formation in and sympathy for the milieu represented by Goswin, and to the lasting influence of his early education.[22]

After further study in Cologne, Panhausen professed at Steinfeld and had several jobs there, including as cellarer, a position of important responsibility in handling the economic affairs of an abbey. Panhausen's capability resulted in the abbots John Schuys de Ahrweiler and Simon Diepenbach giving him many duties. When Abbot Diepenbach succumbed to the plague, Panhausen was elected abbot on November 4, 1540, then confirmed by the abbot general despite the efforts of some secular princes to interfere in the election.[23]

The years immediately preceding Panhausen's accession as abbot of Steinfeld had seen massive losses for the Premonstratensians in much of northern and central Europe. In the kingdom of Hungary, the combination of Ottoman conquest and Protestant inroads had led to the suppression of some sixty-five Premonstratensian communities by 1540.[24] As the Scandinavian kingdoms embraced Lutheranism, all of the Premonstratensian houses there disappeared under government pressure between 1529 and 1538. Like-

---

21. Post, *The Modern Devotion*, 598.

22. Gerits, "Jacob Panhuysen," 13.

23. Valvekens, "Jacobus Panhausen," 110; Gerits, "Jacob Panhuysen," 10–12.

24. François Petit, *The Norbertine Order: A Short History*, trans. and ed. Benjamin Mackin (De Pere: St. Norbert Abbey Press, 1963), 131–32.

wise, the government had suppressed and dissolved all the English and Welsh Premonstratensian houses between 1535 and 1540, with Eggleston abbey the last to be closed, in the year Panhausen was elected abbot of Steinfeld.[25]

Closer to home for Panhausen, the political and religious situation in the Holy Roman Empire had led to the suppression of most religious houses by the time he became abbot. Whenever a German prince embraced the Lutheran reform, religious houses in his territory were dissolved or occasionally transformed into Protestant institutions. Beginning with the seizure of church and monastic lands by Philip of Hesse in 1528, Premonstratensian "circaries," or provinces, disappeared in Hesse, Saxony, Brandenburg, Pomerania, Württemberg, and the Rhineland Palatinate. Some of the women's Premonstratensian houses in Germany carried on as Lutheran institutions for a time, with no formal connection to the Order of Prémontré. Likewise some abbeys became effectively Lutheran collegiate churches, as did the Premonstratensian abbey in Magdeburg. The only Premonstratensian houses that remained in the Holy Roman Empire were in Bavaria, Austria, and the territories of the ecclesiastical principalities—as was the case for Steinfeld in the lands of the prince archbishop of Cologne.[26]

Panhausen was deeply involved in the wider affairs of the Order in those troubled times. The unstable conditions of the period are attested by the inability of Panhausen, like many other abbots, to attend any Premonstratensian general chapter held during his long nearly forty-two-year tenure as abbot. As the general chapter stated as late as 1584, two years after Panhausen's death under General Despruets, "the Chapter has excused the abbots of the circaries of

25. Ardura, *The Order of Prémontré*, 184–87.
26. Ardura, *The Order of Prémontré*, 182–84.

Floreffe, Brabant, and Flanders, Frisia and Germany, be-
cause of wars and letters of excuse sent to the chapter."[27]
The 1549 general chapter made Panhausen vicar general of
the order for the circaries of Westphalia, Wadgassen, Iveldia,
Dacia / Denmark, Norway, Saxony, Poland, Moravia, and
Sclavonia, and renewed the appointment in 1550.[28]

Entrusted with these wide-ranging responsibilities, Panhausen exerted considerable time and effort supporting
monastic reform and the interests of the Order throughout
central Europe. A few examples suffice here. In a surviving
letter of August 13, 1560, King Philip II of Spain entrusted
Panhausen with the reform of the Premonstratensian con-
vent of Houthem-Saint Gerlach, in the province of Limburg,
in the Spanish Netherlands.[29] Later, in 1571, Panhausen led
a successful legal struggle to preserve the ancient rights of
the Frisian abbeys of the Order and prevented their incor-
poration into new diocesan structures.[30] Additionally, he
worked closely with Abbot Jan Meuskönig of Teplá Abbey
in Bohemia in the successful efforts by Meuskönig to reform
the ancient community and strengthen its school.[31] These
successes stand out in a sea of difficulties. The fact that
Panhausen was nominally in charge of the recently suppressed circaries of Scandinavia and northern Germany
must at times have been the source of considerable anxiety,
stress, and melancholy.

Within Germany itself, Panhausen clearly enjoyed the full
confidence of Abbot General Despruets. In a letter dated May
8, 1575, appointing Panhausen as vicar general of the circaries

---

27. Valvekens, "Jacobus Panhausen," 101.

28. Goovaerts, *Ecrivains, artistes et savants*, 2:11–13.

29. Trudo J. Gerits, "Documents inédite sur les visites canoniques de Jean
Despreuts, abbe-general de prémontré au XVIe siècle," *Analecta Praemonstratensia* 44 (1968): 118.

30. Valvekens, "Jacobus Panhausen," 102.

31. Valvekens, "Jacobus Panhausen,"103.

of Westphalia and Ilfeld and giving him the charge to visit monasteries in the dioceses of Mainz and Würzburg, Despruets refers approvingly to Panhausen's "knowledge, faith, and experience of the affairs of our monasteries" (*de tua scientia, fide, rerumque nostrorum monasteriorum experientia*).[32] Panhausen's supervisory efforts helped restore discipline to various Rhenish abbeys in real danger of dissolution due to Lutheran sympathies and pressure.[33]

While a full study of the activities of Panhausen within the Order remains to be completed, this brief sketch demonstrates that he was deeply involved in affairs of the Premonstratensian Order far beyond his immediate duties as abbot of Steinfeld, including its oversight of some seventeen parishes.[34] His extensive responsibilities should be seen as a continuation—now in the highly charged atmosphere of the Reformation and the widespread distress of the Order in northern Europe—of the already extensive activities of the abbots of Steinfeld in this regard in the later Middle Ages.[35]

Despite his extensive external obligations, however, Panhausen did not neglect his own community. As a young abbot in Steinfeld he reorganized the abbey school and determined that the lessons in philosophy and theology should occur on a daily basis. With that goal in mind, he also campaigned for an expanded monastic library. Further, he presided over the final stages of the famed stained glass windows in the Steinfeld cloister and made other material improvements.[36]

---

32. Gerits, "Documents inédite," 118.

33. Gerits, "Jacob Panhuysen," 13.

34. Gerits ("Documents inédite," 18, n. 9) provides references to the relevant manuscript holdings found in Dusseldorf, Staatsarchiv, *Akten Steinfeld*, vol. 2.

35. See Meier, "Die nordwestdeutschen Pramonstratenser angesichts von Verfall und Reform des Ordens 1350–1550," 45–56.

36. Gerits, "Jacob Panhuysen"; William P. Hyland, "The Stained Glass *Biblia Pauperum* Windows of Steinfeld Abbey: Monastic Spirituality, Salvation

Panhausen's intellectual reputation was attested by the great Greek patristics scholar, jurist, and philologist Laurentius Sifanus, professor at Ingolstadt, who among other accomplishments prepared an important edition of the works of Gregory of Nyssa. In 1567 Sifanus fled Cologne because of plague and was given refuge by Panhausen. While at Steinfeld Sifanus prepared an edition and translation of the important Byzantine exegete Theophylactus, and in a letter to Mark and Johanna Fugger he referred flatteringly to the erudition and piety of Panhausen (*virum litteris et pietate et prudentia ornatissimum*) and noted the zeal with which the elderly abbot discussed his scholarly project with him.[37]

The discussion of the two works translated in this volume shows that until the very end of his life, Panhausen remained intellectually active, conversant with the theological trends of the day. After long struggles with illness he died on January 22, 1582, and was buried in the chapel of Saint Mary Magdalene in his abbey church. He was succeeded as abbot by his cousin, Balthasar Panhausen, after a reign of nearly forty-two years and the reception of seventy-four canons at Steinfeld during those tumultuous decades.[38]

The Writings of Abbot Panhausen

Panhausen's writings seem to have been intended primarily for his canons or similar monastic audiences and appear to have circulated in manuscript among various

---

History and the Theological Imagination," in *The Moving Text: David Brown and Biblical Studies in Dialogue*, ed. Christopher R. Brewer, Garrick V. Allen, and Dennis F. Kinlaw III (London: SCM Press, 2018), 143–60.

37. Valvekens, "Jacobus Panhausen," 104; Gerits, "Jacob Panhuysen," 14. Sifanus's letter can be found in *Patrologiae Graecae cursus completus* (PG), ed. Jacques-Paul Migne (Paris, 1841–1864), 125:477–82.

38. Gerits, "Jacob Panhuysen," 14.

Premonstratensian houses. As late as 1768 a manuscript now located in Trier was attested at Steinfeld;[39] Panhausen's writings also survive in a manuscript at Averbode Abbey.[40] They include a treatise on princely rule, a long commentary on the *Rule of Saint Augustine*,[41] a shorter summary and analysis of the Augustinian Rule entitled *Praefatio in Regulam*,[42] a brief biography of Saint Augustine drawn from the *vita* by Possidius and Augustine's *Confessiones*, and short treatises or spiritual conferences given by Panhausen to his confreres on various monastic subjects. Two of these works have been edited by J. B. Valvekens and are the basis of the present translation.[43] Additionally, Panhausen's *Visitationsprotokolle* from the years 1549–1577, with extensive official correspondence, also survives.[44]

Panhausen's writings, although gathered together in well-produced manuscripts, were published neither during his own lifetime nor posthumously by his confreres. The following list of his extant known spiritual and pastoral works is based upon the copies found in Averbode[45] and Trier.[46] It assembles both manuscripts and edited versions with

39. Goovaerts, *Ecrivains, artistes et savants*, 2:11–13.

40. Averbode, Abdijarchief, 4, hs. 330; Trier, Stadtbibliothek, hs. 2199/1818.

41. J. B. Valvekens, "Abbatis I. Panhausen Commentaria in 'Regulam' S. Augustini," *Analecta Praemonstratensia* 54 (1978): 144–65. Valvekens also gives an overview of the opuscula in the Averbode manuscript.

42. William P. Hyland, "Abbot Jacob Panhausen of Steinfeld's *Praefatio in Regulam Divi Aurelii Augustini Hypponensis Episcopi* (1570 Text and Commentary)," *Analecta Praemonstratensia* 94 (2018): 132–59.

43. J. B. Valvekens, "Exhortatio pia abbatis Panhausen, abbatis Steinfeldensis 1572," and "Abbatis Panhausen Tractatus de Monasticae Vitae Cultoribus atque religiosorum votis," *Analecta Praemonstratensia* 54 (1978): 166–90, 191–219.

44. Dusseldorf, Staatsarchiv, *Akten Steinfeld*, 2:179.

45. In Valvekens, "Abbatis I. Panhausen Commentaria," 149–52.

46. For a description of this manuscript and its contents, see Gottfried Kentenich, *Beschreibendes Verzeichnis der Handschriften der Stadbibliothek zu*

secondary scholarship referenced in notes. Well-established dates follow the relevant title in brackets. Since the Averbode manuscript is specifically dated to August 29, 1575, we can be assured that all the *opuscula* contained in it are no later.[47] This leaves open the possibilities that the works unique to the Trier manuscript are indeed later than 1575 and that Panhausen was actively writing or compiling until his death in 1582. Or perhaps they were simply not included in the Averbode manuscript. It is difficult to determine whether dates recorded in the copies represent when the individual texts were composed or copied, or whether some were composed earlier. On the one hand, the securely founded dates for Panhausen's writings on the *Rule of Saint Augustine* (1570–1573) indicate that they are a product of intensive effort in the wake of the Council of Trent to follow the conciliar directive for regular religious to receive instruction in their particular rules and traditions. On the other hand, it is very likely, although impossible to prove, that many of Panhausen's writings on moral subjects are composites of spiritual conferences he gave over many years, with the form in which we have them now representing the elderly abbot's final versions. Further study on the life and career of Abbot Jacob Panhausen may reveal additional evidence for a more specific chronology of his writings.

Panhausen's Known Works

1) *Vita praeclarissimi et incomparabilis Ecclesiae Doctoris D. Aurelii Augustini . . . etc.* [ante 1575]
Mss.: Averbode, Abdijarchief, IV, hs. 330, fols. 1–10ᵛ; Trier, Stadtbibliothek, hs. 2199/1818, fols. 1–11.

Trier, Sechtes Heft. Ascetishe Schriften, 2 Abteilung, Nachträge (Trier: Kommissionsverlag der Fr. Lintzchen, 1910), 157–58.

47. Valvekens, "Abbatis I. Panhausen Commentaria," 148.

2) *Praefatio in Regulam Divi Aurelii Augustini Hypponensis episcopi.* [1570]
Mss: Averbode, Abdijarchief, IV, hs. 330, fols. 11–17ᵛ; Trier, Stadtbibliothek, hs. 2199/1818, fols. 46–54. Edition: William P. Hyland, "Abbot Jacob Panhausen of Steinfeld's *Praefatio in Regulam Divi Aurelii Augustini Hypponensis Episcopi* (1570 Text and Commentary)," *Analecta Praemonstratensia* 94 (2018): 132–59.

3) *Commentarii in regulam D. Aurelii Augustini Hypponensis episcopi, etc.* [1573]
Mss: Averbode, Abdijarchief, IV, hs. 330, fols. 19–184ᵛ; Trier, Stadtbibliothek, hs. 2199/1818, fols. 55–238.

4) *Annotationes breves seu verius collationes scriptarum correspondentium in regulam B. Augustini, etc.* [1573]
Mss: Averbode, Abdijarchief, IV, hs. 330, fol. 186–212; Trier, Stadtbibliothek, hs. 2199/1818, fols. 12–45.

5) *Ad praelatos et subditos pia exhortatio.* [1572]
Mss: Averbode, Abdijarchief, IV, hs. 330, fols. 213–24ᵛ; Trier, Stadtbibliothek, hs. 2199/1818, fols. 267–90. Edition of Averbode manuscript: Fr. Jean-Baptiste Valvekens, "Exhortatio pia abbatis Panhausen, abbatis Steinfeldensis 1572," in *Analecta Praemonstratensia* 54 (1978): 166–90.

6) *Carmen lugubre ad Deum Patrem optimum maximum.* [1572]
Ms: Averbode, Abdijarchief, IV, hs. 330, fols. 225ᵛ–26. Edition: Fr. Jean-Baptiste Valvekens, "Abbatis I. Panhausen Commentaria in 'Regulam' S. Augustini," *Analecta Praemonstratensia* 54 (1978): 151–52.

7) *De commiseratione erga proximum, dilectione atque eleemoysna.* [ante 1575]
Mss: Averbode, Abdijarchief, IV, hs. 330, fols. 227–43; Trier, Stadtbibliothek, hs. 2199/1818, fols. 310–33.

8) *Tractatus de monasticae vitae cultoribus atque religiosorum votis, etc.* [ante 1575]
Mss: Averbode, Abdijarchief, IV, hs. 330, fols. 244–64; Trier, Stadtbibliothek, hs. 2199/1818, fols. 239–66. Edition of Averbode version: Fr. Jean-Baptiste Valvekens, "Abbatis Panhausen Tractatus de Monasticae Vitae Cultoribus atque religiosorum votis," in *Analecta Praemonstratensia* 54 (1978): 191–219.

9) *Tractatus quod murmur et detractio abominatio sunt coram Deo et hominibus, inde de mandacio et septem peccatis compendiose in ordine redactis.* [ante 1575]
Mss: Averbode, Abdijarchief, IV, hs. 330, fols. 264^v–74^v; Trier, Stadtbibliothek, hs. 2199/1818, fols. 291–308.

10) *Quam sit pestifer et execrabilis animus immodice pertinax.*
Ms: Trier, Stadtbibliothek, hs. 2199/1818, fols. 339–59.

11) *De infelici eorum exitu, qui deum potestatemque ab ipso ordinatam vilipendunt.*
Ms: Trier, Stadtbibliothek, hs. 2199/1818, fols. 360–413.

12) *Quam sit homini christiano utilis et pernecessaria frequens mortis et extremi iudicii memoria.*
Ms: Trier, Stadtbibliothek, hs. 2199/1818, fols. 437–59.

13) *De principe et magistratu, qui munere et officio sibi delegato in malum abutuntur, etc.* [1581]
Ms: Trier, Stadtbibliothek, hs. 2199/1818, fols. 419–33.[48]

14) *De sacramentali confessione.*
Ms: Trier, Stadtbibliothek, hs. 2199/1818, fols. 464–68.

---

48. A brief summary of this text is found in Bruno Singer, *Die Fürstenspiegel in Deutschland im Zeitalter des Humanismus und der Reformation: Biblographische Grundlagen und ausgewählte Interpretationen* (Munich: Wilhelm Fink, 1981), 125–26.

15) *Carmina hexametrica.* [1572 and 1576]
Ms: Trier, Stadtbibliothek, hs. 2199/1818, fols. 460–62.

Detailed analysis of *A Loving Exhortation to Prelates and their Subjects* and *Treatise on Monastic Life and Religious Vows* follows below, but here a few general characteristics of Panhausen's writing require mention. As Valvekens has pointed out, we glean very little autobiographical information from Panhausen's spiritual conferences.[49] The abbot's discussion of the problems of monastic administration as distracting from the spiritual life, although representing a motif extending back to at least Pope Gregory the Great, may directly reflect his own long experience as abbot, as could his discussion of abuses and his spiritual and pastoral wisdom on how to overcome them.

Panhausen's Latin style, vocabulary, and rhetoric owe nothing whatsoever to medieval scholasticism, instead echoing biblical, patristic, Cistercian, and contemporary humanistic vocabulary and rhetoric. He writes in the first person, usually addressing his audience in the second person plural. Likewise, he often alludes to or directly quotes classical authors, among others Sallust, Plutarch, Horace, Terence, and Ovid, for rhetorical effect and didactic purposes. His writings offer no indication that he has read Greek sources in the original. Except for an occasional mention of patristic sources, usually Augustine, Panhausen rarely cites an earlier monastic authority by name. This selectivity is undoubtedly partly due to his works' genre, the spiritual conference, but it also reflects the fact that over many decades the abbot has drunk deeply from the tradition of regular religious life. At almost every turn he has clearly synthesized biblical and earlier monastic tradition

49. Valvekens, "Abbatis I. Panhausen Commentaria," 150.

in ways that are virtually seamless—natural to him. The following quotation from the Jesuit William Harmless about Saint Bernard of Clairvaux might also be applied to Panhausen:

> In reading Bernard, we need to remember that he was a monk and spent some hours each day practicing the monastic discipline of *lectio divina,* or sacred reading, that slow, meditative chewing over sacred words, whether from the Bible or from Church Fathers. The careful reader can hear a hundred voices behind Bernard's, the way he subtly absorbed phrases from Augustine or Gregory the Great, from the Psalms or the Gospels or St. Paul. But Bernard's works are neither pastiche nor patchwork. The voice is always his own, yet within it or under it there are haunting echoes of more ancient voices.[50]

Similarly, Panhausen's spiritual teachings are the product of deep immersion in Sacred Scripture; biblical texts, particularly the Psalms and New Testament, are the foundation of his teaching. His biblical quotations are often from the Vulgate, but, significantly, he also uses Erasmus's New Testament paraphrases. As with his other quotations from Erasmus, for instance from *Adages,* Panhausen quotes without citation. He also utilizes published works of contemporary German theologians of his generation. As the analysis below of two of his *opuscula* indicates, Panhausen has much in common with and should be placed among the German Catholic Pauline reformers who, like him, preceded and spanned the period of the Council of Trent. His Christocentric biblical orientation and penchant for using the language of moderate reformers, who themselves had much in common with the early Lutherans, may well have

---

50. William Harmless, *Mystics* (New York: Oxford University Press, 2008), 47.

seemed old-fashioned and perhaps uncomfortable to the next generation of his confreres in the very different post-Tridentine context. This discordance might help explain why—despite the careful collection and preparation of his works in at least two manuscripts during his latter years, and despite the spiritual depth of his traditional teaching and his own impeccable orthodoxy and recognized zeal for reform—Panhausen's writings were left unpublished by his confreres. Now, building upon the important work of Valvekens and others, the study below allows this eloquent and learned Norbertine reformer once again to speak to a receptive and appreciative audience.

A Loving Exhortation to Prelates and their Subjects

Form and Content

Panhausen's *Loving Exhortation* appears to be a collection of spiritual conferences, perhaps originally composed separately but in their extant form assembled by the author into a coherent whole. The text's transitions between different topics,[51] whether simply rhetorical devices or revealing the oral origins of the text, reflect its genesis as several distinct addresses. Their intended audience was primarily monastic, if not exclusively Premonstratensian. Panhausen's opening invocation of the *Rule of Saint Augustine* nevertheless locates his text firmly within the life of the Order. Clearly the manuscript in its current form, accompanied by a prefatory note to a reader, is meant to be read privately. Nevertheless, the exhortation and its constituent parts would have been suitable for use in monastic visitations, the chapter house *collationes*, or abbatial lessons of Panhausen's own abbey—even

---

51. See, for instance, para. 6. Hereafter notes refer to this text as *Exhortation*, followed by the paragraph number in the translation below.

for gatherings of the clergy in general. The possibility of the
latter audience is supported by the author's use in the prefatory "letter to the reader" of the term *senatus ecclesiae*, a term
in use at the time for the clergy of Cologne.[52]

Panhausen's *Exhortation* begins with a preface to the reader.
The abbot asserts that while what this conference has to say
is not for everyone, for those who are enmeshed in inappropriate vices, it may explain the error of their ways and encour-
age them to emulate the good so as to emend their lives. The
clergy and particularly those vowed to the religious way of
life have a grave responsibility in this regard. In a beautiful
image, recalling the mirror mentioned at the end of the *Rule
of Saint Augustine*,[53] Panhausen summons his audience to
return to the pristine state that marked their first youthful
embrace of the religious life: "Their way of life should light
the way for the rest, so that others, contemplating this way
of life as if looking at themselves in a mirror, will soon wash
away their stains and remove any wrinkles they detect. Moreover, they should nourish and strengthen what is righteous,
beautiful, and delightful to behold."[54]

The *Exhortation* is essentially a commentary upon Psalm
23:3-4, "Who will ascend the Mountain of the Lord: or who

---

52. The term *senatus ecclesiae*, synonymous with *coetus presbyterorum*, had
been used since at least the time of Saint Jerome to refer to the assembly of
clergy of a diocese whose specific duty was to advise the bishop. See Giulio
Lorenzo Selvaggio, *Antiquitatum christianarum institutiones* (Madrid: Antonio
de Sancha, 1779), 195. John Calvin, a contemporary of Panhausen, would also
use the term in the *Institutes* (book 4, chap. 3, sections 4–9) to refer to the body
of ministers collectively representing different functions within the church.
See Iohannes Calvinus, *Christianae religionis institutio (editio postrema, 1559)*,
col. 782 (Turnhout: Brepols, 2010).

53. *Rule of Saint Augustine*, chap. 8, para. 2. For an English translation, see
Adolar Zumkellner, *Augustine's Ideal of the Religious Life* (New York: Fordham
University Press, 1986), 295.

54. *Exhortation*, prefatory note, para. 2.

shall stand in his holy place? The innocent in hands and clean of heart, who has not taken his soul in vain, nor sworn deceitfully to his neighbor." Panhausen's chosen scriptural text is then developed and articulated as a summary of the religious life.

Appropriately, as a Premonstratensian Panhausen begins with the *Rule of Saint Augustine*, noting the centrality to the rule of the love of God and neighbor, then quickly moving into the proper role of superiors and subjects. He urges, "to this most of all let our discourse run, that through good works we confirm our vocation and election."[55] He then discusses the religious who should desire to climb the holy mountain and arrive at beatitude. They must truly become disciples to do so, he says, for only they may accompany the Lord in his mountain ascents in the various gospel episodes. In emphatically scriptural language, Panhausen emphasizes the joy to be found in this ascent. He eloquently describes the means of ascent to beatitude as a pure heart, cleansed of both exterior and interior base motives and deeds. Here he places himself in a long line of Latin monastics going back to Cassian and Augustine—through the Cistercians and Carthusians—to his own canonical order. He laments how few among contemporary prelates fit this description, noting that each of his small subsequent orations are meant to exhort them to repentance, so that "those superiors whose works ought to so brightly shine forth" may serve as a model so "that religious may compose their own life and habits to follow their image."[56]

The first oration is on the *status* of prelates, reflecting a term used at least since the fifteenth-century conciliar movement to describe those who are in positions of pastoral and

---

55. *Exhortation*, para. 1.
56. *Exhortation*, para. 7.

juridical responsibility in the church.[57] Panhausen reflects on the haughtiness of many who glory in the rank of office but take no delight in its responsibilities. Because they possess a short-term view based upon temporal pleasures, they are hypocrites; Panhausen stresses that such false leaders will not be exempt from the severest eternal punishment. After describing wicked prelates as pestilence and abomination, he lists the baser sins and charges prelates enmeshed in these errors to turn and desist from them immediately.

From there Panhausen moves on to discuss religious superiors who focus too much on the temporal matters of their abbeys. Here he mixes satire with interesting information about the nature of extensive monastic estates, noting that these economic activities easily become a distraction. He affirms that worldly business of the monastery demands appropriate solicitude, but not when such concern takes over and pushes out primary spiritual concerns. Misguided superiors caught up in worldly business embrace titles and honors that Christ himself was ashamed to take up. Additionally, their emphasis on the wealth of the monastery is often to the detriment of the poor, even to the majority of confreres in the house itself. Panhausen echoes the Wisdom literature when he proclaims, "Thus we should become rich by godliness, in the true goods of the soul, and be content with the things that suffice to the necessity of the present life as we hasten toward immortality. To accumulate the types of riches we need not leave behind is a great work."[58]

---

57. For a discussion of this term in late medieval reform, see Philip H. Stump, *The Reforms of the Council of Constance (1414–1418)* (Leiden: Brill, 1994), 249–63; in a specific Premonstratensian context, see William P. Hyland, "Premonstratensian Voices of Reform at the Fifteenth-Century Councils," in *Reassessing Reform: A Historical Investigation into Church Renewal*, edited by Christopher M. Bellitto and David Zachariah Flanagin (Washington, DC: Catholic University of America Press, 2012), 208–30; especially 213–14.

58. *Exhortation*, para. 19.

Ironically, greedy and unscrupulous superiors, while enriching themselves, often leave the fabric of the abbeys in their charge in poor condition, run down, and impoverished. Their misguided priorities lead to a decline in study and other sacred pursuits, leaving the younger religious in a terrible situation, without the guidance of experienced and serious superiors.

Panhausen acknowledges the gravity of the contemporary situation of religious communities, saying that time is running out for reform. While he is undoubtedly also referring to the personal morality and particular judgment of individuals, he must also have had in mind the precarious nature of the whole monastic establishment in Reformation Europe:

> For now the axe has been applied to the tree—not just to the branches or trunk, but to the roots below—and the tree will certainly be felled by an irreparable wound unless worthy shoots are brought forth to God. The imminent and pressing crisis admits no delay. Up to this point whether we wish to embrace safety is still in our hands. The axe will not strike if we will immediately change our mind. But just as there is a common safety for those hastening to embrace it, so there is a common peril for those delaying.[59]

Returning to his scriptural theme, Panhausen teaches that this very embrace of humility will allow religious to continue their ascent of the holy mountain.

Panhausen then begins a new section of his discourse, focusing on the three monastic vows of chastity, poverty, and obedience, respectively, and on the fact that—as the psalmist implies—lack of fidelity to the vows impedes the

---

59. *Exhortation*, para. 25.

ascent of the holy mountain.[60] He addresses strong language to those who violate their vows, but tempers it with mercy and the sound pastoral statement that while he knows that all will err and allow their souls to be weighed down by these sins, there is always a place for mercy, amendment of life, and forgiveness. Panhausen's treatment of obedience is notable for his emphasis on obedience to the abbot, but also for his Augustinian and Benedictine emphasis on life-long stability in a place (*stabilitas loci*). He reinforces the vow of religious obedience with the stress on obedience to secular laws as essential to a healthy commonwealth, making extensive use of Romans 13.

Fear of civic anarchy linked to religious innovation and rejection of hierarchical authority was hardly unique to Panhausen, and the brief Anabaptist takeover of Münster was a preoccupation of Catholic authors and authorities in nearby Cologne.[61] Panhausen's fundamental outlook, supported by many biblical examples of the response of divine justice to human injustice, is that restraint of human behavior by law, including appropriate punishment of violations, is necessary for the survival of any healthy human community.

Panhausen then begins a new discourse "about the virtue of silence, an inestimable treasure as the safeguard of peace and the foundation of religious life."[62] While upholding the Premonstratensian tradition of the importance of edifying speech for the religious life,[63] he proceeds with a long and

---

60. *Exhortation*, para. 27.

61. See Sigrun Haude, *In the Shadow of "Savage Wolves": Anabaptist Münster and the German Reformation during the 1530s* (Boston: Humanities Press / Brill, 2000), 39–69.

62. *Exhortation*, para. 38.

63. For the fundamental articulation of the medieval canonical mission, see Caroline Walker Bynum, "The Spirituality of Regular Canons in the Twelfth Century," in *Jesus as Mother: Studies in the Spirituality of the High Middle Ages* (Berkeley: University of California Press, 1982), 22–58; especially 43–46.

cogent discourse, seamlessly combining biblical and classical wisdom, to describe the detrimental features of a petulant and unrestrained tongue, and inappropriate garrulousness. With characteristic moderation, he distinguishes the benign and healthy joviality of human familiarity and relationships from inappropriate language and jokes and ridicule at the expense of others, and he skillfully presents the traditional psychology of the way this latter vice leads to sin and behavior destructive of individuals and communities. He then goes on to give shorter but no less cogent discourses on lying, slander, verbal abuse, and the desire for revenge, excessive talkativeness, and pride. He closes with a compelling summary of all his major points, and a return to his theme drawn from the Psalmist:

> Since human affairs are both vile and prone to vanity, we must ascend to a greater life and more excellent dignity, and strive at more complete discipline. Indeed, only through these means does the path lie open to that mind of the Lord. If life seems hard to you, unburden yourself; if difficult, do not regret emptying yourself; if tedious, hurry the more; if laborious, cry out: *Draw me: we will run after thee to the odour of thy ointments* (Song 1:3). Happy is he who so runs that he may grasp, rather that he may be grasped and led up to the mountain to the vision of the great God, who is above all things blessed forever. Amen.[64]

Sources and Context

The most important source for Abbot Panhausen is sacred Scripture, and his arguments are fundamentally grounded in biblical examples. In this small work, beginning with his thematic text, he draws Old Testament references most frequently from the Wisdom literature, especially Psalms and

---

64. *Exhortation*, para. 75.

Proverbs. His New Testament sources are wider ranging, with a strong emphasis on Pauline texts, supplemented by the gospels, Acts, and the catholic epistles.

As was noted previously, besides his frequent use of the Vulgate, Panhausen also quotes extensively from the scriptural paraphrases of Erasmus, specifically the Epistle to the Romans and Jude, without citation. Erasmus had composed these paraphrases between 1517 and 1524 and repeatedly revised them. They were essentially rewritings, with commentary and annotations, of the canonical texts, in Erasmus's own elegant Latin style, and they enjoyed a huge popularity among humanists and reformers in the first half of the sixteenth century.[65]

Panhausen's use of these Erasmian scriptural texts (as well as Erasmus's *Adages)* is significant for several reasons. First, it confirms Panhausen's formation and sympathies in a strongly humanistic context. Second, it shows how much Panhausen had internalized the Scriptures through private study, rather than only through liturgical use confined to the Vulgate. Third, it emphasizes that he clearly valued the rhetorical style of the paraphrases in this pastoral and didactic context.

For Panhausen to find Erasmus congenial might seem at first surprising, given Erasmus's well-known criticisms of many aspects of religious life and the fact that he had received a papal dispensation from his obligations as a canon regular of Steyn. However, Erasmus's attitude toward monastic life was more complex than his criticisms would suggest. Erika Rummel has argued convincingly that Erasmus

---

65. See John B. Payne, Albert Rabil, and Warren S. Smith, "The *Paraphrases* of Erasmus: Origin and Character"; R. A. B. Mynors, "The Publication of the Latin Paraphrases," in *New Testament Scholarship: Paraphrases on Romans and Galatians*, ed. Robert Dick Sider, Collected Works of Erasmus, vol. 42 (Toronto: University of Toronto Press, 1984), xi–xxix.

went through several stages in his attitudes toward monastic life and vows, and that his harsher criticisms of abuses—about which later in life he expressed regret—were in reality little different from the calls of reformers like Panhausen (and others likewise influenced by the *Modern Devotion*) for religious to embrace the spirit of their founders and to live in simplicity, faithfulness, and peace.[66] That Panhausen continued to use Erasmian texts, albeit without citation, two decades after the papacy had put them on the Index of Forbidden Books—whether forbidding them outright or, like the *Adages* after 1575, permitting them only in heavily expurgated versions[67]—may well have agitated or indeed embarrassed his younger confreres. Nevertheless, his usage demonstrates his affinities with circles of moderate Catholic humanist reformers whom he quotes elsewhere, for example Julius von Pflug, bishop of Naumburg,[68] who remained loyal to the Roman Catholic Church but had many concerns in common with Protestant reformers.[69]

66. Erika Rummel, " 'Monachatus non est Pietas': Interpretations and Misinterpretations of a Dictum," in *Erasmus' Vision of the Church*, ed. Hilmar M. Pabel, Sixteenth Century Essays & Studies 32 (Kirksville, MO: Sixteenth Century Journal Publishers, Inc., 1995), 41–56.

67. For a discussion of the attempt to ban the works of Erasmus in the mid-sixteenth century, see Paul Grendler, "The Survival of Erasmus in Italy," *Erasmus in English* 8 (1976): 2–22.

68. For Panhausen's citation of Pflug, see Hyland, "Abbot Jacob Panhausen of Steinfeld's *Praefatio in Regulam Divi Aurelii Augustini Hypponensis Episcopi* (1570 Text and Commentary)," 145. For a full treatment of Pflug's career, see Jacques Pollit, *Julius Pflug (1499–1564) et la crise religieuse dans l'Allemagne du XVIe siècle* (Leiden: Brill, 1990).

69. For discussion of the humanistic impulse in German monastic circles, see Franz Posset, *Renaissance Monks: Monastic Humanism in Six Biographical Sketches* (Leiden: Brill, 2005). For the continuous presence of irenic positions in German Catholic circles, see Howard Louthan, *The Quest for Compromise: Peacemakers in Counter-Reformation Vienna* (Cambridge and New York: Cambridge University Press, 1997).

The complexity of the contemporary discourse of reform was evident in events in Panhausen's own archdiocese of Cologne in the years immediately preceding his election as abbot in 1540. Archbishop Hermann von Wied, at first an outspoken opponent of Luther, gradually became very supportive of ecclesiastical reform in the Erasmian sense of proposing correction of corrupt practices and raising of clerical standards, but not doctrinal change.[70] His efforts in this regard are reflected in the detailed canons of a provincial council that met in Cologne in 1536, which were soon published along with an *Enchiridion christianae institutionis*, a handbook of Christian life explaining the Lord's Prayer, Apostles' Creed, Ten Commandments, and seven sacraments.[71]

While the conciliar canons were primarily concerned with the standards of the secular clergy, some of its themes reflected Panhausen's concerns expressed in the *Loving Exhortation*. The descriptions of both the responsibilities and vices of prelates is one such example,[72] as is the decree entitled *Loquacitas vitanda*.[73] The section of the decrees designated *De vita monastica* contains three chapters entitled respectively "On the Conduct and Way of monks [*De vita et conversatione monastica*]," "The Pursuits and Exercises Necessary for Monks [*Monachorum studia atque exercitationes quales esse oportet*]," and "The Necessity to Recall to Confinement Wandering Monks [*Monachos vagos sub custodia revocandos*]."[74] The general tenor of the decrees is to warn against preoccupation with any external matters that would

---

70. August Franzen, *Bischof und Reformation: Erzbischof Herman von Wied in Köln von der Entscheidung zwischen Reform und Reformation* (Münster: Aschendorff, 1971).

71. Among various editions, I consulted *Canones Concilii Provincialis Coloniensis anno celebrati M.D. XXXVI, etc.* (Paris, 1547), hereafter cited as *Canones*.

72. *Canones*, fol. 20.

73. *Canones*, fol. 23.

74. *Canones*, fols. 42–45.

distract monks from their primary purpose of a life centered upon prayer and God. While it is unclear whether Panhausen attended this council as a young canon, he would certainly have been familiar with its proceedings. He would also have been personally acquainted with Archbishop von Wied, who ordained him priest and was present at his installation as abbot of Steinfeld.[75]

The tumult and fluidity of Panhausen's and Steinfeld's local situations is dramatically illustrated by the fact that by 1542 Archbishop von Wied had shifted from advocacy of moderate reform to inviting the Protestant Martin Bucer to introduce radical changes into his local church. These moves, complicated by imperial politics and military intervention by the Emperor Charles V, were heavily resisted by the clergy of Cologne, and eventually von Wied was excommunicated by the pope and deposed as archbishop in 1546.[76] Despite this end to the archbishop's troubled career, a stained-glass window depicting Archbishop von Wied, ironically accompanied by iconography stressing his loyalty to the papacy and Roman Catholic Church, remained in the Steinfeld cloister.[77] His successor, Adolphus von Schaumberg, who later attended the Council of Trent, issued his own synodal statutes in 1549, stressing the need for abbots to remain in their monasteries, and targeting and censuring other clerical abuses.[78] Navigation of these events[79] in the archdiocese of Cologne during Panhausen's first decade as

75. Gerits, "Jacob Panhuysen," 11.

76. For a discussion of Bucer's activities in this regard, see Martin Greschat, *Martin Bucer: A Reformer and His Times* (Louisville, London: Westminster John Knox Press, 2004), 183–206; and Hastings Ells, *Martin Bucer* (New Haven: Yale University Press, 1931), 321–37.

77. Hyland, "The Stained Glass," 154–55.

78. *Statuta Synodalia*, etc. (Paris: apud Audeonum Paruum, 1550), 13–14, 18ff.

79. For a detailed overview, see Norbert Trippen, *Geschichte des Erzbistums Köln* (Cologne: Bachem, 2008).

abbot undoubtedly left a strong impression on Panhausen, and he never lost his zeal for reform in the spirit of the Cologne canons and eventually, later in life, the disciplinary decrees of Trent itself.

Abbot Panhausen's humanistic interests are also evident in his quotation of classical authors, always without citation of the original author. For the most part Panhausen quotes Martial, Ovid, Virgil, Horace, and Varro to support a particular moral point as well as for rhetorical flourish. His most extensive use of a classical author in this regard is Plutarch (ca. 46–ca. 120), one of the great moralists of pagan antiquity, who had been a favorite of Renaissance humanists since the recovery of his genuine works in the fifteenth century.[80] Panhausen's aim in using Plutarch is exemplary, that is, to point out the vice of loquacity as opposed to the virtues of silence and pithy speech. Panhausen thus quotes from Plutarch's *De garrulitate* on several occasions. Plutarch's *Moralia*, which would have been available to him in Latin from a 1532 edition printed in Basel,[81] also provides examples from the rulers of Sparta of the value of few and well-considered words. Panhausen's admonition against the vice of excessive loquacity is reinforced by references to the Christian Scriptures, particularly the Wisdom literature. His overall point, in this and other contexts, is that if the

---

80. Francesco Becchi, "Le traduzioni latine dei *Moralia* di Plutarco tra XIII e XVI secolo," in *Plutarco nelle traduzioni latine di età umanistica (Seminario di studi, Fisciano, 12–13 luglio 2007)*, ed. Paola Volpe Cacciatore (Naples: Strumenti per la ricerca plautrachea, 2009), 11–33. See also the work of Marianne Pade, especially *The Reception of Plutarch's Lives in Fifteenth-Century Italy*, 2 vols. (Copenhagen: Museum Tusculanum Press, 2007). For general discussion of the reception of Plutarch beyond the fifteenth century in various countries, see *A Companion to Plutarch*, ed. Mark Beck (Chichester: Wiley Blackwell, 2014), especially Part 4, 529–76.

81. Plutarch, *Moralia: De placitis philosphorum*, trans. Gulielmus Beda (Basel, 1531).

pagans could display a virtuous restraint of speech, how much more should Christian religious. Panhausen's interweaving of pagan and Christian moral wisdom on the theme of silence and restraint of the tongue was common among the humanists, and it had antecedents in late medieval Germany as well. One example appears in a sermon given by the great reformer and churchman Nicholas of Cusa to the flock of his episcopal see in Brixen on July 20, 1455. Toward the end of the homily, while discussing the requirement for the faithful to imitate Christ in word and deed, Cusanus describes the need to always speak the truth and also to practice restraint of the tongue as fundamental to the Christian life. After citing Bernard and Thomas Aquinas on these matters, Cusanus finishes with a flourish that combines the Epistle of James, Old Testament Wisdom, and the sayings of the Roman Cato (*Dicta Catonis*) in ways very similar to Abbot Panhausen a century later:

> Christ had moderation in speaking, and so [should] you [have]. As a rich man does not spend money unless it is first counted, so let us not speak except with aforethought. Therefore, to our Christian religion it especially pertains to bridle the tongue. For the Apostle James says: "He who esteems himself religious but does not bridle his tongue—his religion is empty." Cato spoke similarly: "I regard the primary virtue to be restraining the tongue." And not without reason do we have one mouth for speaking and two ears for hearing. To have kept silent does no harm; to have spoken causes harm. (Cato) Talkativeness is a sign of foolishness, according to Solomon. Silence is the material of peace. And so, [silence] befits religion. For "by means of very few words a quarrel sometimes grows to be immense." (Cato)[82]

---

82. This is from Cusanus's Sermon 196, *Respice de caelo*, trans. Jasper Hopkins, in *Nicholas of Cusa's Didactic Sermons: A Selection* (Loveland, CO: The Arthur J. Banning Press, 2008), 363–64 and n. 366.

The remarkable similarity of Panhausen's teaching to that of Cusanus here points to their mutual indebtedness to the tendency of patristic and later monastic thought to interweave classical and biblical moral wisdom as complementary. A further example can be found in *A Loving Exhortation*, where Panhausen quotes, without explicit citation, the *Metamorphoses* of the pagan poet Ovid to make clear the relationship of humans' upright posture to human dignity: "And, though, all other animals are prone, and fix their gaze upon the earth, he gave to man an uplifted face, and bade him stand erect and turn his eyes to heaven."[83] While Panhausen here quotes directly from Ovid, his reference calls to mind Bernard of Clairvaux's Sermon 24 on the Song of Songs, where the great Cistercian develops this thought of Ovid in his own theological discourse:

> God indeed gave man an upright stance of body, perhaps in order that this corporeal uprightness, exterior and of little account, might prompt the inward man, made to the image of God, to cherish his spiritual uprightness; that the beauty of this body of clay might rebuke the deformity of the mind. What is more unbecoming than to bear a warped mind in an upright body?[84]

Much in Panhausen's *Loving Exhortation* is reminiscent of Bernard. While Panhausen's rhetorical style incorporates classical techniques, such as the sarcastic exclamations of the comic playwright Terence,[85] he is also clearly influenced

---

83. *Exhortation*, para. 2.

84. Bernard of Clairvaux, *On the Song of Songs II*, trans. Kilian Walsh, Cistercian Fathers 7 (Kalamazoo, MI: Cistercian Publications, 1983), 46. The image of mind-body incompatibility went back to the Church Fathers, for instance, Ambrose, *Liber Unus de Joseph Patriarcha*, cap. 2, Patrologiae Latinae cursus completus (PL), ed. Jacques-Paul Migne (Paris, 1841–64), 14:668.

85. *Exhortation*, para. 17.

by Bernard's famous *Apologia to Abbot William*. In this masterpiece of monastic rhetoric, Bernard roundly criticizes what he portrays as the excesses of life at Cluny, particularly in matters of food and clothing. Like Bernard in this text, Panhausen uses the rhetorical technique of *praeteritio*, in which he asserts his reluctance to speak about a particular issue but then proceeds to do so. Like Bernard in this and his other works, Panhausen asks rhetorical questions of the reader or audience or a fellow religious, and often ends a section by asserting he can say no more. While it is not possible to demonstrate direct textual influence, Panhausen is clearly aware of and inspired by a tradition of monastic style as represented in the writings of Bernard, as well as those of Peter the Venerable and Peter Damian.[86]

In *A Loving Exhortation*, of which the content and style reflect the context of contemporary humanism, as his use of Erasmus affirms, Panhausen also echoes and emulates a reform tradition that has deep roots in the works of eleventh- and twelfth-century regular religious, ultimately Augustine and the Fathers. Jean Leclercq famously described this monastic tradition as characterized by both "rhetoric and sincerity," attracting and engaging the reader in its simplicity: "Artifice is reduced to the minimum; it plays no greater part than that accorded it in ancient rhetoric where eloquence makes sport of eloquence, where technique was never a substitute for inspiration. . . . The element of sincerity accounts for the simplicity which makes these texts so easy, and even agreeable, to read."[87]

---

86. For a discussion of these techniques in Bernard's *Apology to Abbot William* and their parallels in the monastic tradition, see Jean Leclercq, "Introduction" to *Bernard of Clairvaux: Treatises I*, ed. Leclerq, Cistercian Fathers series 1 (Shannon, Ireland: Cistercian Publications, 1970), 15–26.

87. Jean Leclercq, *The Love of Learning and the Desire for God*, trans. Catharine Misrahi (New York: Fordham University Press, 1982), 174–75.

We see then in Panhausen an eloquent expression of a perennial method of interweaving biblical wisdom with pagan moralists—a tradition passed down from the Fathers through the great articulations of medieval monastic reform and utilized by both later churchmen like Cusanus and humanists such as Erasmus. *A Loving Exhortation* reveals this method at work in the private world of chapter house and cloister, as one extraordinary abbot articulated the principles of monastic reform in a time of threat and crisis—but also in the hope and promise of renewal.

Treatise on Monastic Life and Religious Vows

Form and Content

Panhausen's *Treatise on Monastic Life and Religious Vows* is intended not only for Premonstratensians or even regular canons living according to the *Rule of Saint Augustine*, but for all those who live the religious life in community. The abbot explains to his audience how and why religious life was instituted, its source and justification as found in Scripture, and its continuing expression as an ideal form for pursuing a serious Christian life and vocation.

Panhausen takes as his theme 1 John 2:16: "For all that is in the world is the concupiscence of the flesh." His explication begins with the dangers of the world and how one must keep constant vigilance against them, followed by a description of the different categories of sin. He cautions that even those sins that seem trivial—if they are in opposition to divine precepts—can often lead to more serious faults. Eating a piece of fruit in Eden seemed trivial, as did the backward gaze of Lot's wife, but the spirit in which these deeds were done led to disaster in both instances. The treatise follows this observation with a description of the wickedness of the world and the many illusions of its dark pleasures. Panhausen explains that while the world created by God is good, what is meant by the *world* in Saint John's text—to which he himself refers—is "but rather the dishonest desires for those wicked things, in which most people place their happiness."[88]

For the Christian, Panhausen explains, leaving behind the world in the physical sense is not enough in itself. That departure represents a state of mind: "A pure mind rather than a physical location rescues us from depraved desires and the world. For what good does it do to leave behind the world and inhabit an empty desert, when, by a tyrannical domination, malice, anger, envy, hatred, pride, and the rest of that sort hold sway, and human eye inspires greater fear in us than the divine gaze."[89] Nevertheless, Panhausen argues, location does help, as does solitude. The call to separate oneself from the world follows the divine command to pray in secret and the clear example of Christ in seeking solitude to pray. This removal from distraction undoubtedly aids prayer and allows the space to put aside pernicious mental images and submit oneself totally to service of God.[90]

After establishing the importance of solitude, Panhausen turns to the origins of monastic life of both sexes, describing how men and women "were inflamed by zeal and devotion" to leave behind the world and its desires, its empty show and fallacious delights. Inspired by two biblical texts, Matthew 19:29 and Psalm 44:11-12, he says, these Christians went out into deserts and secret places, leaving all behind for God. He explains that the monastic state arose before all patterns of Christian life, saving that of priests. In the moving passages that follow, he provides descriptions of the way

88. *Treatise*, para. 3.
89. *Treatise*, para. 4.
90. *Treatise*, para. 6.

the ancient monks sought solitude, "the nursemaid of contemplation," in pursuit of Christian devotion, to be freer for quiet prayer and concentration. The calm supported by this removal from worldly affairs, he explains, while it always requires vigilance to maintain, draws them toward the crucified Lord of majesty. Here perhaps we hear an echo of Panhausen's frustrations after decades as a busy abbot: "When it comes to those things that concern the senses, every occasion of sin has been taken away. They do not gaze upon women, do not handle money, do not engage in legal suits; insults are not heard among them; they do not buy, sell, invest, make contracts, exchange money. In short, no one causes any trouble for them, nor do they trouble others."[91]

After asserting that monks were numerous in antiquity, Panhausen shifts to the question of vows, saying that ancient monks voluntarily bound themselves by vows to observe the three evangelical counsels of chastity, poverty, and obedience. Returning to his thematic scriptural text (1 John 2:16), he explains how each of these vows helps counter particular vices mentioned in the biblical text, namely desire of the flesh, avarice, and pride. If a religious of his own time practices the humility of heart at the center of these vows and of opposition to all vices, such a one will be "permitted to gaze upon the form of the primitive Church . . . to contemplate those fonts."[92] The battle against vice, Panhausen asserts, is ultimately fought with spiritual weapons. He makes extensive use of military metaphors and Pauline imagery to describe the struggle against the world and sensual pleasures. He explains that the example of the monastic fathers' perseverance in this struggle shows us the grace and power of God, upon whom the Christian life depends. Our struggle is not something about which to despair. On the contrary,

---

91. *Treatise*, para. 10.
92. *Treatise*, para. 13.

looking to ancient witnesses fills us with confidence and hope in God's mercy and assistance. Through the three counsels represented by the vows, we shake off the yoke of the devil and offer ourselves to God in perpetual sacrifice.

Panhausen then moves on to a topic with both deep roots in monastic history and immediate relevance in the context of Reformation Germany. Without naming any specific Protestant reformer, he notes that some have attacked religious vows as contrary to Christian liberty. In blunt language, he asserts that those people are fools who do not see clearly. In a shift to what seems to be a highly personal form of address to his audience, Panhausen then asserts the key part of his argument:

> Listen, my brother in the Lord, I beseech you, listen. Christian liberty in this most of all consists, that a person can either keep a vow or not. For his own judgment has decided whether he wished or did not wish to make a vow. God does not command a vow to be made, but rather to be fulfilled. Indeed, a marriage not yet contracted is not binding. However, when once it will have been contracted it is firm and insoluble, and so necessary that short of a great sin it is not able to be dissolved. And so it is with the vows of religious. When someone, voluntarily and with deliberate intentionality, speaks and confirms a vow by oath, if he does not keep it, the Lord God demands it from the hands of that person himself.[93]

Referencing numerous biblical passages affirming that Scripture teaches that vows are binding, he then concludes powerfully:

> Clearly, then, a vow does not stand against Christian liberty, but rather is its defense and protection. That is what Scripture teaches, nature dictates, and honor commands.

---

93. *Treatise*, para. 27.

Indeed, while it is true that vows do compel ordinary servitude, in the case of religious it is servitude to Christ, and this servitude is the highest liberty. For the Apostle says, *Being then freed from sin, we have been made servants of justice* [Rom 6:18] and God. And further: *Know you that to whom you yield yourselves servants to obey, his servants you are whom you obey, whether it be of sin unto death, or of obedience unto justice* [Rom 6:16]. Therefore none can doubt that chastity, poverty, and humble obedience, according to numerous passages from the Scriptures, are pleasing to God. Who, unless weak of mind, and deprived of common sense, does not embrace these virtues with both arms? To seek after false light in the middle of a clear day is absurdly misled. Those who do so are withered branches on the tree, diseased members in the body, a bear in the vineyard, a wolf among sheep.[94]

Having affirmed the validity and dignity of religious vows and the vocation they support against its detractors, Panhausen stresses that religious profession in itself is no guarantee of salvation or sanctity. Indeed, he argues, religious should not think their salvation, or justice, which only comes from God, should be sought after by rule, profession, vestments, ceremonies, or any external things. He proceeds to discuss how we attribute justice (*iustitia*) to Christ alone, and mentions the twofold justice acknowledged by the monastic fathers. First is the justice attributed to Jesus alone, which we embrace by faith. A second justice—the justice we call human—God also demands from us, namely to observe the things commanded in the Decalogue. No one, Panhausen warns, however that individual may be justified, should judge himself to be free from the observance of the commandments. We go on from day to day, as the Apostle

94. *Treatise*, paras. 29–30.

says, mortifying the members, employing the weapons of sanctification.

After this detailed treatment of justification Panhausen stresses how, despite the criticisms of adversaries, religious know that diverse rules and habits and cowls do not make a monk. Citing the famous opening sentences of the *Rule of Saint Augustine*, he asserts that what matters most is being of one heart and one mind on the way to God. When this ideal is at the center of life, why not allow a monk, according to his ancient custom, to be allowed to do the same? Some say keeping vows is impossible, and humanly speaking this may appear to be so. But, Panhausen asserts, it is God who works this fidelity in us all through grace, and we must stand upright and let God strengthen us.

With these fundamental points in place, Panhausen then proceeds to discuss in more detail, through extensive quotation of the Bible and fathers, that each of the three vows, or evangelical counsels, counters particular vices. Chastity he describes as a safer life than marriage, but, as in all his arguments, he stresses that this virtue must be voluntarily embraced: each must decide for himself if he is called to this way of life. Interestingly, Panhausen warns that celibacy is no panacea: there is such a thing as a chaste marriage and marriage bed without stain, and there is also virginity that is impure. Each person must discern for which life he is fit, then fully embrace it.

Poverty, again, must only be taken up voluntarily. Panhausen asserts that "poverty of spirit is the root and foundation of the whole of the Gospel, and indeed of Christian truth."[95] He elaborates persuasively on poverty as key to the *imitatio Christi*, and he expands upon the poverty of Christ with many New Testament references. For the

95. *Treatise*, para. 51.

apostles, he says, poverty was voluntary upon their being called to discipleship. By its example poverty condemns disordered priorities, and religious who do not embrace it—both literally and in correct disposition of mind—should be ashamed. He points out that the apostles, indeed all Christians of the nascent church, followed this path. Much of the last part of his treatise is given to describing the vice of greed and excessive desire for possessions and worldly comforts. The rejection of avarice helps avoid concupiscence, and avarice and zeal for becoming rich are fatal preoccupations.

Finally, Panhausen turns to the vow of obedience, which alongside humility he describes as the epitome of all other virtues. Without humility to oppose pride, nothing can be acceptable before God. Obedience, he explains, was the path of humility taken up by the ancient monks, who like the apostles followed Christ both by word and example. The Scriptures demonstrate the dire consequences of pride in many examples, in Lucifer, David, and countless others. The arrogant, he concludes, can find no rest for their hearts.

In a lovely passage, Panhausen summarizes how the three vows arm devotion and renew the spirit in its struggles. Without interior charity, he concludes, the lowest step of religious life is never achieved. Paraphrasing Saint Jerome, he urges his audience to stay faithful to this path once taken, to take a stand against the world and its false enticements, and to oppose all the vices that can undermine charity:

> We must not lack charity, the bond of perfection and summation of the law. Without it every virtue is imperfect, and chastity, poverty, obedience—in the end all our acts of justice—will be as dust, which the wind[96] blows from

---

96. Valvekens omits *ventus*, found in Averbode.

the face of the earth. Happy that man whose heart the
love of Christ and charity have wounded with a sharpened spear. Charity alone offers a living person to God
as a victim and acceptable sacrifice. This makes true religious, this makes monks, without this monasteries are
hells and those dwelling in them demons. But indeed, if
this charity is present, monasteries are *paradises of pomegranates* [Song 4:13] and *lilies of the valleys* [Song 2:1] on
the earth, and those living in them are angels.[97]

Sources and Context

While an abbot's giving spiritual conferences on the
meaning of the vows and religious life is not exceptional in
itself,[98] the need to explain and justify the framework for
religious profession clearly took on an added urgency for
Abbot Panhausen in the context of Reformation Germany.
Obviously his tract is not a polemical work intended primarily to convince a literate Protestant audience. He makes
only oblique references to the Protestants, and never by
name. The point of his discussion is rather to exhort his
brethren and confirm their resolution to remain faithful to
their vows. In this sense, his treatise is akin to the works on
which Caroline Bynum focused in her study of the spirituality of the regular canons in the twelfth century—works
of private spiritual instruction intended for fellow religious
rather than an element of public polemic.[99]

---

97. *Treatise*, para. 79.
98. For the earliest Premonstratenisan example, from the twelfth century,
see Adam of Dryburgh, *Liber de ordine habitu et professione canonicorum ordinis
praemonstratensis*, PL 198:439–610. For Panhausen's contemporary, Premonstratensian Nicholas of Psaume, see Ardura, "Les exhortations," 26–69.
99. See Bynum, "The Spirituality of Regular Canons," 22–58.

In his approach Panhausen reflects the atmosphere of monastic humanism in his primarily scriptural and Christo-centric emphases, adverting occasionally to classical and patristic authors. He is careful, in light of Protestant criticisms, to take into account a nuanced view of grace and justification, as will be discussed below, carefully reflecting controversial theological debates as summarized by the contemporary German Franciscan Conrad Kling and also at the Council of Trent. His *Treatise on Monastic Life and Religious Vows* focuses on the monastic life and religious vows in general, not specifically those of Premonstratensians or regular canons. Panhausen addresses how and why religious life was instituted, and clearly perceives a true similitude between the monks and regular canons. The great battles over which way of life—that of the canons regular or the monks—was superior, a conflict generating much heat and anger in the twelfth century, finds no echo here beyond a brief mention that clerics predate monks in the history of the church.[100]

In choosing the scriptural theme from 1 John 2:16, Panhausen in fact closely follows the example of his great teacher, Saint Augustine, who gave a series of sermons on this epistle. Although he does not seem to be quoting Augustine verbatim in this treatise, Panhausen does echo, in his discussion of what is meant by the world, Augustine's homily on these verses.[101] Like Augustine, Panhausen is clear to stress that the world in the sense of creation is good in itself, but that its dangers and forms of concupiscence are the central moral problem.[102]

---

100. *Treatise*, para. 8.

101. See Augustine's *Homily II on I John*, paras. 11–14; see also as translated by H. Browne, *Augustine of Hippo, Works*, ed. Philip Schaff, Nicene and Post-Nicene Fathers, First Series, vol. 7 (Buffalo, NY: Christian Literature Publishing Co., 1888).

102. *Treatise*, para. 3.

Beyond this shared choice of scriptural theme, Panhausen is more generally shaped by Augustine's ideals of the religious life as expressed in his Rule and other writings. Central for Panhausen as for Augustine is the idea that the religious life must be rooted in the virtue of charity. Augustine uses many metaphors drawn from Scripture, and particularly from Paul's letters, to describe the monastic life as the ever-progressing renewal of God's image within us. The perfection of Christians living in wisdom is the perfection of love, so the forsaking of possessions and the preservation of virginity, obedience, and other such gifts are of no use to those who receive them if they lack love. Poverty and humility are central to the imitation of Christ. The language of *holy warfare* is relevant for all Christians, just as *servitude* expresses the complete dependence of the faithful on God. What differentiates the monk's duty from the ordinary Christian's is that the monk offers such service free from all worldly bonds. Augustine is always at pains to stress that this gift is a free servitude, undertaken with no compulsion by free men under grace, unlike servitude under the Law. A religious must gladly renounce the attachments represented by the vows and with an open heart for it to have meaning. The evangelical counsels, like all virtues, counter particular vices. All appropriate asceticism and moral discipline must be inextricably linked to charity, and obedience freely undertaken makes regular religious persons more like Christ.[103]

All of these Augustinian teachings on the monastic life are reflected in Panhausen's *Treatise on Monastic Life and Religious Vows*. His deep dependence on the teachings of Augustine is fitting for a Premonstratensian abbot who in following the Augustinian rule strove to guide his community and

---

103. For a detailed discussion of Augustine's influence in these ideas, see Zumkellner, *Augustine's Ideal of the Religious Life*, 103–34.

instantiate *religio Augustini* in its own corporate life. Panhausen supplements his dependence on Augustine by references to Jerome and Ambrose, and also to pagan authors of antiquity such as Ovid and Philostratus. This literate and humanistic approach, fusing scriptural and patristic authors with the moral rhetoric of antiquity—and the absence of scholastic terminology and dialectic in his arguments—places Panhausen squarely in the tradition of *docta pietas*. This theological modality, the union of wisdom and piety with eloquence, characterizes a style of religious writing and devotional attitude based upon biblical and patristic models. While Panhausen may indeed demonstrate an affinity with Erasmus and other contemporary humanists, he is best understood within a specifically monastic tradition, as is well exemplified in the work of the Italian monk Ambrogio Traversari (1386–1439). As practice and written representation, *docta pietas* was thriving in Panhausen's own day, within the monastic orders of Germany as elsewhere in Europe.[104]

---

104. For an overview of Traversari's adherence to the ideal of *docta pietas*, see Charles Stinger, *Humanism and the Church Fathers: Ambrogio Traversari (1386–1439)*, and *Christian Antiquity in the Italian Renaissance* (Albany: SUNY Press, 1977). For a detailed discussion of Traversari's application of humanist ideals in his monastic life, see Costanzo Somigli and Tommaso Bargellini, *Ambrogio Traversari, Monaco Camaldolese: La Figura e la Dottrina Monastica* (Camaldoli: Edizioni Camaldoli, 1986). See also Patrizia Castelli, "Lux Italiae: Ambrogio Traversari Monaco Camaldolese: Idee e Immagini nel Quattrocento Fiorentino," *Atti e memorie dell'Accademia Toscana de scienze e lettere: La Columbaria* 47 (1982): 39–90; William P. Hyland, "The Climacteric of Late Medieval Camaldolese Spirituality: Ambrogio Traversari, John-Jerome of Prague, and the Linea Salutis Heremitarum," in *Florence and Beyond: Culture, Society and Politics in Renaissance Italy*, ed. David S. Peterson with Daniel E. Bornstein (Toronto: Centre for Reformation and Renaissance Studies, 2008), 107–20. On monastic humanists contemporary to Panhausen, see Posset, *Renaissance*.

Discussion of the legitimacy and purpose of the classic vows of chastity, poverty, and obedience lies at the heart of Panhausen's text. Lifelong commitment to religious life was, in the lived experience of historical and contemporaneous religious, expressed through the profession of solemn vows after several years of simple and probationary vows. By the thirteenth century, the ancient vows of obedience and stability in lifelong fidelity to the abbot or other prelate and a specific religious rule—as well as commitment to chastity and personal poverty—were normally discussed in terms of the three vows, particularly in writings of friars. The mobile ministry of the friars naturally resulted in their view of obedience being focused on their respective rules and particular order, not lifelong stability in a particular abbey. The threefold grouping of vows as poverty, chastity, and obedience became for all religious the normal way to talk about the vows.

The eleventh and twelfth centuries had seen bitter debates over which way of life was better, or more perfect—the orders of hermits, monks, or canons regular. The *Apologetic Letter* of Anselm of Havelberg (d. 1158) is perhaps the best-known Premonstratensian contribution to this discourse. Anselm argued 1) for the temporal priority of the regular canons over the monks, 2) that the vocation of the canons as clerics was essential to the life of the Church in the way that the vocation of the monks was not, and 3) that the mixed life of action and contemplation led by the canons was more difficult than the life of the monks and in fact the most authentic way to imitate the example of Christ.[105] However, all of the protagonists in the twelfth-century

---

105. For a translation and commentary, see *Norbert and Early Norbertine Spirituality*, ed. and trans. Theodore J. Antry and Carol Neel (Mahwah: Paulist Press, 2007), 29–62.

debate among the orders assumed the legitimacy of religious vows in the life of perfection.

Assumptions regarding the character of regular religious orders began to shift in the thirteenth century with the rise of the mendicant orders. The entry of the friars into urban and university life—and tensions arising between them and secular masters at the universities—had roused many opponents to the friars' way of life, especially to their vow of poverty. This dispute led important mendicant theologians, such as the Dominican Thomas Aquinas, to defend and explain religious vows. For example, in *Summa Theologica*, Aquinas devotes twelve articles to the nature of vows, the necessity of their being voluntary, and their binding nature. In doing so he cites Augustine and numerous scriptural passages, many of which would be used in subsequent debates and by Panhausen himself.[106] Additionally, again drawing heavily upon Augustine, Aquinas discusses the life of Christian perfection in terms of the perfection of charity.[107] A contemporary of Aquinas, the Franciscan Bonaventure, provided extensive discussion of the vows and evangelical counsels in such works as *Disputed Questions on Evangelical Perfection* and *Defense of the Mendicants*.[108] Issues surrounding monastic vows continued to be a subject of heated controversy. The fourteenth-century Englishman John Wyclif (d. 1384) and his followers also attacked mo-

---

106. Thomas Aquinas, *Summa Theologiae* (Rome: Leonine Commission, 1948), IIa-IIae, q. 88. For a standard English translation, see *Summa Theologica of St Thomas Aquinas*, trans. Fathers of the English Dominican Province (New York: Benzinger Brothers, 1948).

107. Aquinas, *Summa Theologiae*, IIa-IIae, q. n184, a. 3.

108. Bonaventure, *Disputed Questions on Evangelical Perfection*, ed. and trans. Thomas Reist and Robert J. Karris (St. Bonaventure, NY: Franciscan Institute Publications, 2008); Bonaventure, *Defense of the Mendicants*, ed. and trans. Jose de Vinck and Robert J. Karris (St. Bonaventure, NY: Franciscan Institute Publications, 2010).

nasticism and religious vows as being essentially hypo-critical and unwarranted by Scripture. Both these authors and those who answered them served as background for Reformation critics as well as for Catholic defenders of regular religious life.[109]

Although recent research has demonstrated the indebtedness of the early Reformation to the reform work and humanist scholarship of many members of religious orders, including Luther's own Observant Augustinian friars,[110] it remains indisputable that—as the Reformation progressed—a key feature of its theology was an explicit attack on the nature and validity of monastic vows. Martin Luther's ultimate rejection of the monastic life is well known. Although his complete rejection of religious vows has been recently recast as a more gradual process than was previously believed,[111] Luther's main arguments were already present in his 1521 treatise on the subject, *The Judgment of Martin Luther on Monastic Vows*. Luther argues here, on the basis of his doctrine of justification by faith, that vows that contradict

---

109. Ian Christopher Levy, "Wyclif and the Christian Life," in *A Companion to John Wyclif*, ed. Levy (Leiden: Brill, 2006), 293–364, especially 295–302; in the same volume, see Mishtooni Bose, "The Opponents of John Wyclif," 407–55.

110. For the importance of the Erfurt *studium* of the Observant Augustinians as background for Luther, see Adolar Zumkellner, *Erbsünde, Gnade, Rechtfertigung und Verdienst nach der Lehre der Erfurter Augustinertheologen des Spätmittelalters*, Cassiciacum vol. 35 (Würzburg: Augustinus-Verlag, 1984). See also Franz Posset, *The Front-Runner of the Catholic Reformation: the Life and Works of Johann von Staupitz* (Burlington, VT: Ashgate, 2003), especially 325–31, for Staupitz's nuanced views of monastic vows in the context of his continuing friendship with Luther.

111. For this process and the intellectual antecedents of Luther, see Heiko Oberman, "Martin Luther contra Medieval Monasticism: A Friar in the Lion's Den," in *Ad fontes Lutheri: Toward the Recovery of the Real Luther: Essays in Honor of Kenneth Hagen's Sixty-Fifth Birthday*, ed. Timothy Maschke, Franz Posset, and Joan Skocir (Milwaukee: Marquette University Press, 2001), 183–213.

this teaching (*justificatio sola fide*) are impious and should not be kept. He did not at this stage condemn monastic life as such, but he said that it could be easily perverted and that it was in his day almost universally pernicious. Luther acknowledges that Scripture does warrant the taking of vows. The question as he defines it is which vows are truly vows—how one can distinguish false from true vows.

Luther's argument in 1521 has five main points. First, he asserts, monastic vows are not commanded by God's word but are contrary to it. To go beyond what Christ commands is sin, not faith. All are called to fulfill vows in spirit as part of the Christian life. The understanding of these vows as expressed and modeled in historical and contemporary monasticism is, however, superficial and external, having nothing to do with true faith. Second, Luther contends, monastic vows conflict with faith. The taking of perpetual vows is a type of righteousness through works, hence antithetical to the Gospel. Third, the compulsory and perpetual nature of monastic vows is a violation of Christian freedom. While for Luther monastic life is permissible if led voluntarily and with a conscience free from works righteousness, it must be chosen freely and is in itself not superior to other ways of life, for instance being a farmer or mechanic. Fourth, monastic vows violate the first commandment and are a type of idolatry. Faith gives way to works and monastic founders are elevated over Christ, he says. Vows often impede and seemingly exonerate the universal Christian responsibility to aid one's neighbor. Fifth, vows are contrary to common sense and reason. People can be dispensed from every vow but celibacy, and that vow particularly torments body and soul.[112]

---

112. For an excellent summary, followed by an edition of the source, see *The Judgment of Martin Luther on Monastic Vows*, in Luther's Works, Volume 44: The Christian in Society, Vol. 1, ed. James Atkinson (Philadelphia: Fortress Press, 1966), 245–49.

In 1526 Luther published the much shorter *An Answer to Several Questions on Monastic Vows* specifically to answer scriptural arguments in favor of monastic vows. He asserts here that reference to Old Testament vows is pointless, as the Mosaic law was abrogated by Christ and that at any rate these vows were temporary, having nothing to do with monastic vows. Luther proceeds to analyze various Old Testament and New Testament texts, specifically arguing that the gospel and Pauline texts so often cited in favor of monastic vows are really about the Christian life in general and in no way justify or have anything to do with later monasticism.[113]

These and similar statements of Luther were affirmed and developed in the foundational Protestant statement of faith known as the *Augsburg Confession* (1530), which in its Article 27 attacked monastic vows without countering any of the longstanding scriptural justifications, rather, producing a few scriptural quotations in favor of the need to marry, procreate, and not to be alone. This article additionally made the point that a person was not justified by religious vows.[114] The Lutheran criticism of vows was answered by the *Roman Confutation of the Augsburg Confession*, which used Scripture in its defense of religious vows while calling for a reform of monastic discipline.[115] Luther's close friend Philip Melancthon, a more systematic theologian than Luther, answered the Catholic response's specific points in his *Apology for the Augsburg Confession*,[116] and as time passed

---

113. Martin Luther, *An Answer to Several Questions on Monastic Vows*, in Luther's Works Volume 46: The Christian in Society, Vol. 3, ed. and trans. Robert C. Schulz (Philadelphia: Fortress Press, 1967), 141–54.

114. For a translation of Article 27 of the *Augsburg Confession*, see *The Book of Concord: The Confessions of the Evangelical Lutheran Church*, ed. and trans. Theodore G. Tappert (Philadelphia: Fortress Press, 1959), 70–80.

115. In *The Augsburg Confession, A Collection of Sources*, ed. J. M. Reu (Fort Wayne, IN: Concordia Theological Seminary Press, [n. d.]), 349–83.

116. For a translation of the relevant article see *Apology of the Augsburg Confession* in *The Book of Concord*, 268–81.

these arguments against religious vows became a central part of Protestant criticisms of the whole Catholic system of supposed works righteousness. This "frontal assault" of the Protestants, as Heiko Oberman puts it, went far beyond the call for reform, and now portrayed monasticism and its vows as a symbol of all that was wrong with medieval Catholic theology and life, and the antithesis of genuine Christian liberty.[117]

Luther's assault on monastic life meanwhile had provoked immediate response, with religious of various orders defending the scriptural basis of monastic vows while simultaneously continuing to work for reform and to articulate monastic spirituality.[118] Many monastic writers, such as the Benedictine Louis de Blois, also known as Blosius (1506–1566), contributed to the defense of intentional religious communities.[119] By Panhausen's time as abbot, in his region of Germany the Carthusians of Saint Barbara's in Cologne had become leading defenders of Catholic doctrine and practice against Lutheran and other Protestant attacks. They expressed their response primarily through many publications, by contemporary Carthusians and others, so helping Cologne maintain its reputation as "a citadel of Catholicism" in the Rhineland.[120] Among these Carthusians special men-

117. Heiko Oberman, "Martin Luther contra Medieval Monasticism," 188.

118. For a comprehensive list, see *Katholische Kontroverstheologen und Reformer des 16. Jahrhunderts: ein Werkerzeichnis*, ed. Wilbirgis Klaiber (Münster in Westfalen: Aschendorff, 1978).

119. See Lambert Vos, *Louis de Blois, Abbé de Liesses (1506–1566): Recherches bibliographiques sur son oeuvre* (Turnhout: Brepols, 1992).

120. See Sigrun Haude, "The Silent Monks Speak Up: The Changing Identity of the Carthusians in the Fifteenth and Sixteenth Centuries," *Archiv für Reformationgeschichte* 86 (1995): 124–40; *Die Kölner Kartause um 1500*, ed. Werner Schäfke (Cologne: Kölnisches Stadtmuseum, 1991); Joseph Greven, *Die Kölner Kartäuse und die Anfänge der Katholischen Reform in Deutschland* (Münster in Westfalen: Aschendorff, 1935); Gérald Chaix, "Réforme et Contre-

tion could be made of the eloquent sermons of the eminent spiritual writer Johann Lansperg (1489–1539), known as Lanspergius, in defense of the monastic life and the need for reform.[121] It is worth noting that Lanspergius dedicated one of his most influential writings, *A Letter of Jesus Christ to a Faithful Soul*, to the Premonstratensian sisters at Hensberch.[122] Undoubtedly Panhausen was in touch and perhaps worked with the Carthusians at Saint Barbara's, knew their library, and closely followed their writings on monastic reform.

Panhausen's *Treatise on Monastic Life and Religious Vows* drew specifically on another German religious and prominent theologian, the Franciscan Konrad Klinge, or Klingius.[123] Klinge had once been at the university of Erfurt, and among his writings, he published shortly before his death in 1565 a book entitled *Loci communes theologici*.[124] This volume was a collection of sermons for the whole liturgical year, but also a systematic treatment of theological points in contention at the time, in which Klinge would present— as he put it—the positions of the heretics and then the

Réforme Catholiques: Recherche sur la Chartreuse de Cologne au XVIe siècle," *Analecta Cartusiana* 80 (Salzburg: Institut für Anglistik und Amerikanistik, 1981).

121. See Greven, *Die Kölner Kartäuse*, 27–49; Gérald Chaix, "La reception du Chartreux Lansperge: Survivance ou métamorphose de la Devotio moderna," in *Historia et Spiritualitas Cartusiensis, Acta Colloquii Quarti Internationalis*, ed. Jan De Grawe (Saint-Etienne: Centre Européen de Recherches sur les Congrégations et Ordres Monastiques, 1983), 59–68.

122. For a translation of this dedicatory letter, see John of Landsberg, *A Letter from Jesus Christ to the Soul that Really Loves Him*, ed. and trans. John Griffiths (New York: The Crossroad Publishing Company, 1981), 23–25.

123. For Klinge's career and bibliography, see Ernst Pulsfort, "Klinge, Konrad," *Biographisch-Bibliographisches Kirchenlexicon* (Herzberg: Verlag Traugott Bautz GmbH, 1992).

124. For editions of this work, five of which were published in Cologne in Panhausen's lifetime, and other writings of Klinge, see Klaiber, *Katholische Kontroverstheologen und Reformer des 16. Jahrhunderts*, 68.

Catholic response. One section of this long work contained a discussion in defense of monasticism. Although he does not mention Klinge by name, Panhausen quotes his *Loci communes theologici* verbatim in his own defense of monastic vows. Likewise, he quotes without citation Klinge's remarks, including the controversial term *duplex iustitia,* on the correct understanding of the controversial doctrine of justification.[125]

Panhausen's use of Klinge's work is telling. Klinge was a fierce opponent of many Lutheran doctrines and for decades helped keep alive Catholic teaching and practice in the fraught religious situation in Erfurt.[126] But as Ernst Pulsfort notes, the Franciscan was nevertheless seen as one of the so-called "Expectanten," those Protestants—most importantly the ex-Dominican Martin Bucer—and Catholics who were attempting and hoping, despite other real differences, to reach a consensus on the central issue of justification, with special attention to the concept of a *duplex iustitia,* or twofold justification.[127] Panhausen's use of this work of Klinge to explain correct Catholic doctrine to his confreres shows that his irenic heart remained with an older group of German Catholic Pauline reformers, among them Klinge, von Pflug, and Johannes Gropper.[128]

---

125. See *Treatise,* paras. 31–34.

126. R. W. Scribner, "Civic Unity and the Reformation in Erfurt," *Past and Present* 66 (1975): 29–60; Nikolaus Paulus, "Conrad Kling, ein Erfurter Domprediger des 16. Jahrhunderts," *Der Katholik* 74 (1894): 146–63.

127. Ernst Pulsfort, "Klinge." For a reassessment of these reformers and their discussions on justification, see Brian Lugioyo, *Martin Bucer's Doctrine of Justification: Reformation Theology and Early Modern Irenicism* (Oxford: Oxford University Press, 2010).

128. As Professor Alexander Ferrer Mitchell of St. Andrews put it in 1892, in discussing these Catholic reformers in Germany, "A fourth author of the same school may be named, who was supposed to come so near in some things to the Reformers, that for a time a report gained currency that he had gone

In a similar vein, Panhausen's *Treatise* made reference to two passages from a work by the Carolingian monk Smaragdus of Saint-Mihiel (ca. 760–840) entitled *Summarium in epistolas et evangelia*.[129] This idiosyncratic choice takes on added meaning when it becomes clear that Panhausen must have accessed this text through its publication as a sermon postil published by the Lutheran Kaspar Hedio in 1536 and appearing in four more editions by 1556.[130] John Frymire asserts that this is the only known medieval postil published by a Protestant during the early decades of the Reformation.[131] Hedio's and other postils published by Protestants could indeed be found in Catholic libraries, and were extensively utilized by Catholic reformers in Germany, as Frymire describes particularly those whose discourse—shaped by the Cologne statutes of 1536—shared many Lutheran attitudes on grace and salvation and ecclesiastical reform.[132]

Panhausen's writings then seem to mark him as a moderate Catholic reformer who used his learning and intellect to build bridges with early Protestantism while upholding central Catholic and monastic principles. The ultimate failure to reach concord between German Protestant and Catholic reformers and the subsequent permanent disunity and century of religious warfare should not obscure the importance of those who labored earnestly to avoid that sad eventuality. Nor should moderates who worked for

over to them, like Monhemius who at first occupied the same standpoint. This was Conrad Cling, or Clingius, of the Franciscan monastery at Erfurt." See Mitchell's preface to the facsimile *The Catechism set forth by Archbishop Hamilton, printed at St Andrews 1551* (Edinburgh: W. Paterson, 1892), x.

129. See *Treatise*, para. 46, para. 69.

130. John M. Frymire, *The Primacy of the Postils: Catholics, Protestants and the Dissemination of Ideas in Early Modern Germany* (Leiden & Boston: Brill, 2010), 455.

131. Frymire, *The Primacy of the Postils*, 508.

132. Frymire, *The Primacy of the Postils*, 263–88.

compromise and mutual understanding in eras of turmoil and controversy be dismissed as unclear thinkers and timid, vacillating figures. Despite the fact that the irenic attitude of Panhausen and others did not carry the day, the voices of those who worked for peace and were willing to acknowledge common ground and the validity of opposing arguments were needed then, and they would appear to be more necessary than ever in the churches and world today.

Panhausen clearly saw his own task as effectively and intelligibly extending a wide circle of monastic reform and Catholic renewal to the canons in his charge, as buttressed by the clarifications of the Council of Trent on doctrine and reform. A careful reader of his *Treatise on Monastic Life and Religious Vows* will find its affirmation of the religious vocation argument sensitive to Protestant concerns and criticism. For Panhausen, there is no sense that monastic vows in any way guarantee or cause justification. Much discussion of Pauline texts and serious attention to anti-Pelagian concerns appears in his works alongside strong affirmation of traditional forms of religious life as appropriate responses to the saving work of Christ on the cross.

While the vowed religious life, Panhausen argues, is the safest environment in which to pursue the Christian life, he does not disparage other ways. In the end, central to Panhausen's defense and articulation of religious vows is Augustinian teaching on love of God and neighbor as the heart of monastic life. For Panhausen, the community of charity embraced by those taking monastic vows means nothing if it is not undertaken as a response in charity and freedom to the scriptural call to holiness.

Notes on Translations

The first edition of any of Panhausen's writings, surviving until the twentieth century only in manuscript, was made by the well-known Premonstratensian scholar J. B. Valvekens. His editions of the two opuscula translated in this volume are based upon a manuscript found in Averbode Abbey as Abdijarchief, IV, hs. 330.[133] The manuscript includes various writings of Panhausen.[134] It is written in a fine humanistic hand, with the text extending across the whole page, with no columns. Another copy of the same works is found in Trier, Stadtbibliothek, hs. 2199/1818.[135] A critical edition of Panhausen's *opera omnia* remains a desideratum.

Valvekens' published transcription of the two opuscula is the basis of the present translation. I have provided punctuation and a numbered paragraph structure while following the capitalization of the manuscript, relocating section titles from the margins into the main text and rendering them in boldface. While scholars of the order owe an immense debt to the erudition and scholarship of Valvekens, his transcriptions' occasional shortcomings are rectified here. Source identifications added below have led to correction of some of those errors.

In general, Abbot Panhausen does not name his sources directly. Biblical quotations and direct quotations from other sources are here identified as much as possible and italicized, with the references provided in the footnotes. Notes also include suggestions about possible further sources. Biblical translations generally follow the Douay-Rheims

---

133. Valvekens, "Exhortatio pia abbatis Panhausen, abbatis Steinfeldensis 1572," 166–90; "Abbatis Panhausen Tractatus de monasticae vitae cultoribus atque religiosorum votis," 191–219. I am grateful to Herman Janssens, archivist of Averbode Abbey, for providing me with a digital copy of this manuscript.

134. For a list of these works in the manuscript, see Valvekens, "Abbatis I. Panhausen Commentaria," 149–50.

135. For a description of this manuscript and its contents, see Gottfried Kentenich, *Beschreibendes Verzeichnis der Handschriften der Stadtbibliothek zu Trier. Sechtes*, 6:157–58.

translation of the Vulgate unless indicated in notes. At times Panhausen himself is clearly following another version than the Vulgate text—or simply paraphrasing or alluding to the biblical text. My text below is the first translation of these opuscula or any of the works of Abbot Panhausen into English. Bernard Ardura had translated a few passages into French in his discussion of Panhausen, and in turn these were translated from French in the English-language edition of his survey of Premonstratensian history by Edward Hagman,[136] but the version presented here is my own.

All translators face decisions about fidelity to the original, balancing accuracy and literal conformity with the need to express in English the clarity of style and forcefulness. In these works, the affectionate familiarity expressed toward the audience of the original Latin adds further challenge. My hope is to make the intimacy of these spiritual conferences come alive for the modern reader, and to render due justice to the intention and style of Abbot Panhausen as a mature and experienced reformer and spiritual teacher at the height of his powers.

---

136. Ardura, *The Order of Prémontré*, 199–201.

A Loving Exhortation to Prelates and Those in Their Charge

To the Beloved Reader:

1. I do not wish those things that I am about to say about the state of prelates and those in their charge to be understood as being about everyone, friendly reader—only about some. Nor do I criticize any one person on this account, although I desire that any delinquents will remedy their faults once they have been admonished. Why should I rail at anyone? It is foolish to wish to dismiss all things that have been prudently instituted for the failings of some. Further, no one is able to complain bitterly about me if I focus on vices, for a general discourse touches no one except him who has previously confessed and recognizes himself to be guilty. When he has done this, it suits him to follow better things, not to find fault with the sins of others.

2. Therefore I exhort you with the affection of Christ that each one of you acknowledge his own dignity, turn away from vices and scandals, and truly emulate the better spiritual gifts. Nothing in human affairs excites the mind of men more to the pursuit of piety and worship of God than the sincere way of life and unblemished behavior of those who have been placed on high as visible to all. To this place those who have already said farewell to this worthless world with

all its pomp—who have indeed delivered their entire selves to the service of God—should especially look up. Prominent among these are religious, prelates, devout clerics, and the favored rank of monks. Their way of life should light the way for the rest, so that others, contemplating this way of life as if looking at themselves in a mirror, may soon wash away their stains and remove any wrinkles they detect. Moreover, they should nourish and strengthen what is righteous, beautiful, and delightful to behold. On this account, it is wholly proper that a cleric who has been called to the service of the Lord should be a complete stranger to every type of vice, to direct his life and behavior to this calling. Not even the slightest offense ought to mar him, but every saying from his mouth should be seasoned with salt. In walking, standing, and all motions of the body, nothing should offend the sight of anyone—but let there be only what befits sanctity. Let clerics exert their influence by integrity of character, so that they may deserve to be called the "senate of the Church."[1]

3. But let us lay aside these matters and look to what remains. Flourish, most beloved reader, and consider thoughtfully whatever is good in this work. For above all, our discourse strives to spare persons and speak frankly about vices. He who is able, let him grasp this and exult in the Lord.

> Our little books learn to preserve this rule,
> To spare the persons, speak to the vices.[2]

---

1. For the history and use of this term, see Introduction, n. 52.

2. Martial, *Epigrams*, X:33. See Martial, *Epigrams, Volume II: Books 6–10*, ed. and trans. D. R. Shackleton Bailey (Cambridge, MA: Harvard University Press, 1993), 2.348–49.

A loving exhortation to prelates and those in their charge, based upon the words from Psalm 23, *Who will ascend unto the Mountain of the Lord*, and so forth, in which various abuses and vices of both prelates and their subjects receive comment.

1. The Rule of the Blessed Bishop Augustine revolves principally around two things beyond love of God and neighbor—the rule of the superior, and the obedience and reverence of those in his care. Therefore it concerns the practice of both prelate and subject. But because among both ranks awareness of abuses generally prevails, few entirely fulfill the duty of their own office, while many are truly estranged from the good and are directed toward evil. Therefore we must say a few things concerning these men. But because *in many things we all offend* (Jas 3:2)—prelates as well as subjects, old men and youths, together as one the rich man and the pauper—and *no man layeth it to heart* (Isa 57:1),[3] to this most of all let our discourse run, that through good works we confirm our vocation and election. Indeed, in doing these things we will never sin, and rather will we be conducted abundantly into the eternal kingdom of our Lord and Savior Jesus Christ.

Of what sort those ought to be who desire to ascend the mountain of the Lord

2. Foremost we must know the means by which we may arrive at the life of eternal beatitude. The royal psalmist—that man whom the Lord found to be according to his own heart—asks a lovely, sweet question about this matter, inquiring, *Who shall ascend into the mountain of the Lord, or who shall stand in his holy place?* (Ps 23:3). All of us strive to

---

3. This scriptural reference evokes the opening of the *Tenebrae* responsory: *Ecce quomodo moritur iustus, et nemo percipit corde.*

ascend, we all stretch toward the heights, and we all aspire upwards. Indeed, a certain author says, "And, though all other animals are prone, and fix their gaze upon the earth, he gave to man an uplifted face, and bade him stand erect and turn his eyes to heaven."[4]

3. To that highest place, therefore, let us be eager to ascend—where it is good that we are there,[5] where it is secure, whence we may not fall. For so the prophet exhorts us, exclaiming, *Get thee up upon a high mountain; thou that bringest good tidings to Zion* (Isa 40:9). If we would ascend this mountain, let us follow Christ not by actual physical footsteps but by lofty deeds, so that we ourselves can be mountains: *Mountains are round about it, so the Lord is round about his people* (Ps 124:2).

4. Seek in the Gospel, and you will discover that only his disciples ascended mountains with the Lord. Happy that man who has laid out the ascent of this mountain in his own heart, desiring and dying to himself in the courtyard of the Lord, as one whose heart and flesh exult in the living God! Certainly that mountain—a fertile mountain, a mountain most overflowing, an abundance of all good things and eternal happiness—is the house of God. *Blessed are they that dwell in thy house, O Lord: they shall praise thee for ever and ever* (Ps 83:5). Somewhere it is written that "*there all pain, sadness, and weeping will flee, where the saints will shine as the brightness of the firmament, and they that instruct many to justice, as stars for all eternity* (Dan 12:3). *For there will be found a joy that eye hath not seen, nor ear heard, neither hath it entered into the heart*

---

4. Ovid, *Metamorphoses* 1.85. See Ovid *Metamorphoses*, trans. Frank Justus Miller (Cambridge, MA: Harvard University Press, 2014), 1:8–9. See the introduction (n. 84) for the use of this Ovidian trope by Bernard of Clairvaux and Ambrose of Milan.

5. The phrase evokes the words of Peter at the transfiguration; see Matt 17:4.

of man (1 Cor 2:9), *unless of those who are found worthy of it, the names of whom are written in the book of life."*[6]

5. Would that we would furl the sails of iniquity and impiety, so that it might be granted to us to remain there forever! Not only does the prophet thus proclaim the desire to go up this mountain, but he truly teaches how those desiring to ascend should make their way. Thus he lays out the conditions of the question he has raised, saying, *The innocent in hands and clean of heart, who hath not taken his soul in vain, not sworn deceitfully to his neighbor* (Ps 23:4). This means the one who has innocent hands and does not harm others at all by his action—who also possesses a pure heart purged from the filth of sins, who does not puff up his own soul to vanity or long for vain and transitory things, much less to deceive a neighbor by perjury. Whoever this one may be, without a doubt he will ascend that very mountain.

6. But who will boast that he has clean hands, or a heart righteous and chaste? *Who can say, my heart is clean, I am pure from sin* (Prov 20:9)? Who will openly dare to profess such a thing? Not even the infant who is but one day old upon the earth! We are *a generation pure in their own eyes, and yet not washed from their filthiness* (Prov 30:12). From this follows another passage: *blessed is that man not in whom sin is not found, but to whom the Lord has not imputed sin* (Rom 4:8). If any such man exists, he is indeed great.

7. For if it may be permitted to probe and examine more deeply, in this day and age, what prelates—or what religious, who live in the full sight of men, and are thus obliged

---

6. This quotation appears to reference a sermon attributed to Bede, *Sermo 18 De sanctis,* which was read in the monastic Office over several days of the Octave of All Saints at Matins. The text of the whole sermon can be found as *Homily 70* among Bede's works in PL 94:450B–52C. Some of PsBede's wording from the excerpts used by Panhausen echoes that found in the Latin translation of Origen, *Homilies on Numbers,* PG 12:750D.

to be the light of the church—may he be found with pure heart and with innocent hands? Alas, the pain! How extremely rare is the number of these, and with the Wise Man I will dare to say that *far and from the uttermost coasts is their price* (Prov 31:10). I am silent about myself and those similar to me, the ones who better know the task of overseers of estates than even the first syllable of how to be a learned and pious abbot. About these our first discourse (*oratio*) will be concerned, namely those superiors whose works ought to shine forth so brightly that religious may compose their own life and habits to follow their image.

On the State[7] of Prelates

8. Some wander far from their duty when they have first been promoted to the status of a prelate, then later begin to grow haughty. Some of them consider themselves to have been elevated to so distinguished a level of honor that they defer to none. Furthermore, they consider themselves to be holier than the one to whom they are superior in rank. In fact, upon their promotion they have experienced merely a change of rank, not of spirit. Some reckon that their delights are under thorn bushes, keeping secret the sins they commit day by day. Thus they grope around in shadows, staggering upon a slippery path. Such men tolerate the heavy yoke of sins, conceal an even heavier conscience, and finally await the heaviest sentence: *Depart into eternal fire* (Matt 25:41). Hence that vessel of election Paul laments that upon us *shall come dangerous times. Men shall be lovers of themselves, covetous, haughty, proud, blasphemers, disobedient to parents, ungrateful, wicked, without affection, without peace, slanderers,*

---

7. Valvekens supplies this heading, which is absent from the Averbode manuscript. On the technical meaning of *status* in this context, see the Introduction, n. 57.

incontinent, unmerciful, without kindness, traitors, stubborn, puffed up, and lovers of pleasures more than of God, having an appearance indeed of godliness, but denying the power thereof (2 Tim 3:1-5). Weeping with the Apostle, I say that *they are enemies of the Cross of Christ, whose end is destruction, whose God is their belly, and whose glory is in their shame* (Phil 3:18-19).

9. For they do not wish to imitate the life and death of Christ so that they may live with him in eternity. Instead, they teach others to pray and fast for profit and their own glory, with the result that while others carry burdens, they themselves in the meantime rule over them and live pleasantly, just as if after this life they fully expect there to be no other. Just as through temporary afflictions we strive toward immortal happiness, so those men claim for themselves eternal ruin through momentary pleasures; they consider the belly in place of God, and through a counterfeit glory among men—which they ground in shameful business—they hasten toward eternal disgrace. Anything terrestrial is temporary and counterfeit, but whatever is true and eternal is celestial, yet such men care about nothing but terrestrial matters. In these they place glory, in these pleasures, in these their own hopes—wandering far from the true evangelical goal. For they have a taste for worldly things, despising official duty, and they rejoice in those things that it is an abomination to name—indeed they exult in the very worst of them.

10. But let us also speak about those superiors who do not move even a finger with regard to fasts, prayers, and the rest of the acts of piety and duties of religion, but their hands are busy with iniquities. Their right hand is burdened by gifts, and, it must be said—even worse—they are not zealous to please God, whom instead in many ways and aspects they gravely offend. Their kingdom is nourished by vices and surrounded by shameful scandals. Their towers are crimes, and their weapons great undertakings of any

sort of baseness they can find, so they disgrace their own office even as they do injury to their inborn nature. Such evil certainly spreads more than is just, and a kind of pestilence takes possession of innumerable men so that, for the glory of this world, they sign a personal pledge of subjection to the devil. They buy pleasure by abomination and the things they desire by wickedness. Their love of lucre asserts itself, while the desire of gain fails to spare the life of a neighbor. Ambition *sleepeth under the shadow, in the covert of the reed, and in moist places. The shades cover his shadow, the willows of the brook shall compass him about* (Job 40:16-17).

11. Do not those daily banquets, those courses at table, those prostitutes, those riches testify to an insatiable desire for malice? Consider closely that whenever you fornicate you condemn yourself. For[8] sin is such that as soon as it befalls, the judge brings sentence. Are you a drunkard, do you indulge the belly, have you plundered? Halt your step now, turn into a different path! Thank God that he has not borne you away in the midst of sins, and so do not seek[9] further privilege in order that you act wickedly. Many have caused damage to others in one moment, then suddenly perished, departing to a manifest judgment. Be afraid lest you suffer this fate without excuse!

12. Some prelates display the outer appearance of humility and are vehemently zealous about the faults of others. In this way, they can appear to thirst and hunger for justice. If only they also exercised the same judgment about their own sins and faults! They foolishly flatter themselves just as much as they shamelessly and inanely burn with indignation against others. Nor do they suffer themselves to be admonished by others, so little do they desire to be corrected. If these men truly desire to be cleansed, they should

8. Averbode *ita*; Valvekens *ibi*.
9. Valvekens omits; Averbode *quaerere*.

not be irritated when they have thus been corrected, but should rather return the greatest thanks to those who place their faults before their very eyes.

On the Household Affairs of Certain Prelates

13. Some prelates take as their sole care—here I set aside pleasure and excess among the majority—collecting the produce of the monasteries with great earnestness. And this becomes the foremost solicitude and preservation of monastic life, that the money boxes are returned and the leather money bags swell with red coins. Yet not at all content with this, they take the greatest pains that the fish ponds be profitable—some abundant with tadpoles, others overflowing with big fish. From here such a prelate's attention goes out into the woods, so felling some trees that will bring profit, while keeping trees bearing acorns for the nourishment of pigs and the shelter of wild beasts, lest they run off into the neighbors' lands and the prelate's own household not have the opportunity to hunt. Many hounds and a great, lazy mob of servants are devoted to this detestable task. If servants be lacking, then peasants are drawn in, to the neglect of their duties. In like manner swarms of bees and their beehives are cultivated, well cared for, and nourished to great profit and for the kitchen.

14. And then we note similar solicitude about administering landed estates, that the cattle may be abundant and profusely provide milk, cheese, and butter—that calves grow strong, cattle grow large, some to supply meat for daily feasts and others for sale to stuff the abbatial money satchel. The same care is given to acquire and tend horses, goats, pigs, sheep, geese, chickens, and the rest of the domestic animals. Here the exercise of agriculture never ceases. This certainly marks a zealous abbot—that the fields are manured, plowed, harrowed, and planted, then too that

the ditches are dug and trenched, small streams are directed in order that numerous streams give rise to the richest fruit in the field as in the meadow, so that indeed orchards and each rural enterprise may be profitable. The vine is yet another preoccupation of abbatial zeal.

15. Surely we need not disregard these economic matters, but only if such excessive solicitude does not interrupt the work of God. Furthermore, things acquired with appropriate and moderate attention need to be faithfully distributed for the use of the brethren and paupers. This ought to be the highest care. But our discourse is not about those who act appropriately, but rather about those who—after they have collected abundant wealth in their concern to acquire things—indulge themselves excessively. They hold in contempt the very people whom they ought to be helping and, neglectful of their own obligations, raise themselves above the very precepts of God. They are disdainful of being called "reverend fathers" but rejoice when men hail them as "rabbi" and are gratified to be named "lords." What more can be established about them but that they usurp cursed and forbidden titles against the will of Christ the Savior? In fact, lest we be called too tactful, Christ himself forbade them.

16. Others have been so completely enslaved[10] by their own passions and worldly matters that they seem unable to be torn away or separated from those distractions. While such men indulge their own conveniences and advantages beyond what is just, as we mentioned above, their subjects suffer. While the brothers are worn out by fasting, hunger, thirst, and cold, these prelates lead a pleasant and delightful life. Indeed, they run riot and gratify their own spirits by every kind of pleasure, maintaining daily banquets as lavish

---

10. Averbode *addicti*; Valvekens *affecti*.

as those others enjoy on feast days, as if dining on slaughtered sacrificial victims.

17. Is it for this reason, O[11] Prelates, that the most excellent founders of churches expend their own goods—so that you may direct them solely to your own advantage, or better yet, I should say, for you to spend upon your own desires? Not the least bit in the world![12] As that herald of divine grace Paul the Apostle says, *Let a man so account of us as of the ministers of Christ*, not lords, *and the dispensers of the mysteries of God* (1 Cor 4:1-2), and as ones who pay out a loan from another, not squanderers or unjust watchmen of his goods. Now it is generally acknowledged that the resources they administer—even the loftiest, the treasury of the church and of paupers—belong to others. When it comes to the actual value of these, nothing should be viewed in any way other than as goods entrusted to them by God to be distributed in good faith, not looking toward anything other than the honor and glory of Christ.

18. But I move on. You should not view all prelates as tainted if they are truly devoted to[13] the adornment of the altar, for to maintain the goods of the altar and to maintain oneself are indeed allowed. But to be haughty, to swell with pride, to be idle in drunkenness and luxury—that is not at all allowed, for heaven's sake! Whatever prelates retain for themselves from the goods of the churches—whatever they consume immoderately beyond necessary food and clothing while others meanwhile are in need—is a type of robbery more serious than any sacrilege. A certain wise man prayed not for superfluous things, but only for those necessary for

---

11. Averbode *O*; Valvekens *non*.

12. The rhetoric of these two sentences echoes the comic poets, for instance Terence, and is meant to be reproachful and sarcastic.

13. Averbode *deserviunt*; Valvekens *inserviunt*.

his sustenance,[14] that is, *having food and wherewith to be covered* (1 Tim 6:8).

19. Thus we should become rich by godliness, in the true goods of the soul, and be content with the things that suffice for the necessity of the present life as we hasten toward immortality. To accumulate the riches we need not leave behind is a great work.[15] Why should we be anxious about collecting riches not really our own, which soon we must leave to others? Just as we brought nothing of these things with us when we came into this world, so when we die we will take nothing with us. To waste wealth on pleasures is a plague—to preserve hoarded possessions is madness. Enormous is the profit when we cast away money to augment the treasure chest of godliness. Enormous too is the loss when, for some paltry gain in this life, we lose immortal riches. Zeal for wealth and zeal for godliness are not compatible. A certain holy man, while begging for necessary things from the Lord, said, *If God shall give me bread to eat, and raiment to put on . . . the Lord shall be my God* (Gen 28:20). Note: he does not pray to God for pride or lasciviousness.

20. Why say more? I am not easily able to draw myself and my mind from these matters, for we are so constituted by nature that if something is very painful it always hovers before the eyes.

21. We who have been honored walk away from the good things of the Lord when we do not bear him honor. We are ministers of Christ, yet we serve Antichrist and mammon when our leggings and sandals shine and glitter more than the altars of churches. For this reason, now abbeys and monasteries are not duly tended, but rather are deprived of goods. The flock entrusted to them is not protected but mis-

---

14. See Prov 30:7.

15. Averbode *Magnum est eas opes accumulare, quae nos nunquam relicturae sunt;* Valvekens *magnum opus est accumulare quae non nunquam relicturae sunt.*

erably lost—not shepherded but devoured, not supported but exposed to shame. As the Lord says through the Prophet, *those who devour my people as if eating bread* (Ps 13:4). *This is a generation which has swords for teeth*, Solomon says, *and grindeth with their jaw teeth: to devour the needy from off the earth, and the poor from among men* (Prov 30:14). Hence many monasteries are left deprived and denuded of their possessions, so becoming miserable and wasted.

22. For such reasons as these we desire to be and indeed are prelates of the churches. But we attain the rank of ministry without the zeal for it. Few desire to be imitators of the good, but solely the heirs of goods. We rejoice in meals, pomp, jesting, games, and dice. There is revelry and feasting, and who does not know the rest? But we must fear lest *mourning taketh hold of the end of joy* (Prov 14:13). For while we, pampered fathers, massage ourselves with these ointments, what will the sons do? Will they not do what they see the parents doing? Certainly, most certainly! From any parent comes offspring like him, and creatures run with their own kind. While a prelate splendidly feasts and abundantly drinks, an impudent youth drains his own cups. This one tosses dice, and that one plays the numbers. *The people*, one says, *sit down to eat and rise to play* (1 Cor 10:7).

23. No serious consideration is given to sacred literature, or anything else from books other than the most recent poison, which those who are rightly the leaders of the flock should abhor. And then, as it is said, like lips, like lettuce,[16] subjects are ignorant of every necessary literary skill. When you put subjects on an equal footing with superiors when they are too immature for freedom, then luxury and apathy gain mastery in their hearts, and these same subjects begin

---

16. A proverb attributed to Marcus Crassus, when he saw an ass eating thistles, quoted by Saint Jerome in Epistle 7.5, suggesting that "like has met its like." See *Epistola 7 Ad Chromatium, Jovinum, et Eusebium*, PL 22:341.

to love vices and live corruptly. Where does this seed come from? From that one who undoubtedly planted the seedling. O lid fitting to its jar! Does not this fearsome voice sound in your ears, O esteemed fathers: *But he that shall scandalize one of these little ones, it were better for him that a millstone should be hanged about his neck and that he should be drowned in the depth of the sea* (Matt 18:6). The supreme Father, most loving of all, spoke to us in these words through his only Son: *So let your light shine before men* that contemplating your life—in every way pure, faultless, and clearly celestial—*they may glorify your father who is in heaven* (Matt 5:16), to whom ought to be all honor and glory.

24. But you should have no other care than to exercise in good faith the office that has been most seriously delegated to you. Then that One whose glory you serve will repay you abundantly with a great reward in his own time. Do not listen to these words, *Drink and be inebriated, my dearly beloved* (Song 5:1), live sweetly, *and under every elbow sew cushions* (Ezek 13:18). Do not expend the Lord's goods, which he generously put under the care of his own soldiers as they set off for a foreign country, on your own desire. Instead call out, *But yet that which remaineth, give alms: and behold all things are clean unto you* (Luke 11:41). For while you support lovely statues more than men, and play pipes and flutes, will not your sons also lead dances?

Such repetitions have nothing in common with the word *order* besides the use of the same word. Among corrupt habits—in places where anything whatsoever is permitted—can there be any place for any piety, regular observance, or finally any monastic discipline, religious life, even a life of integrity or character? Where the reins are carelessly let loose, there religious are inclined on their own to every kind of vice. What sadder, more calamitous thing can be imagined? In the very places where so many holy men through many years cultivated piety and all monastic discipline with the highest praise and edification of neighbor, now is all to be disturbed by a few scoundrels? O misery of miseries, to be reduced to ash by eternal fires!

25. Now we speak of heavy matters, but a graver judgment remains. Return therefore to the heart and do not fall asleep, dearest ones. Now extreme danger presses, and the whole matter is on a razor's edge. Sincere souls must either enter the kingdom of heaven or face eternal punishment. Salvation is at hand for those who embrace it, but punishment and incurable destruction also lie at hand for those who refuse. For now, the axe has been applied to the tree—not just to the branches or trunk, but to the roots below—and the tree will certainly be felled by an irreparable wound unless worthy shoots are brought forth to God. The imminent and pressing crisis admits no delay. Up to this point, the question of whether we wish to embrace safety is still in our hands. The axe will not strike if we will immediately change our mind. But just as there is a common safety for those hastening to embrace it, so there is a common peril for those delaying. It seems to me that I might see some sign of our justification if in our dealings with others we always strove for humility. For this is the road by which we ascend on high to the mountain, concerning which our Lord spoke to us, saying, *He that humbleth himself shall be exalted* (Luke 14:11).

26. The great splendor of justice, constituted for others more than for itself, sustains community and society. Indeed it sits on high, so that it holds all things subject to its own judgment, carries wealth to others, collects money, does not refuse duties, undertakes strange dangers. Who would not desire to hold this place of virtue unless avarice had weakened and indeed warped the vigor of so great a virtue? And indeed, when we desire to increase riches, accumulate money, take over lands with possessions, or display wealth,

we have put off the form of justice, lost the common benefit of doing good. But what does that wise man say? *Delay not to be converted to the Lord, and defer it not from day to day. For his wrath shall come on a sudden, and in the time of vengeance he will destroy thee* (Sir 5:8-9). Certainly we do not know what that unexpected day will bring forth, but there is danger and anxiety if we put off conversion, and certain safety if we act immediately. Therefore, let us cultivate virtue so that, though we die, we will depart in safety. But now it is time to put an end to these discussions. I will place a guard over my mouth, lest in speaking so many things hastily, my tongue misspeak.

On the State of Certain Religious

27. Now we must look at the life of religious and monks, asking whether or not they have over time undertaken their way of life in vain, and in making their vows[17] have sworn falsely to their superiors, rendering their promised fidelity useless, with the result that something is able to keep them from ascending that illustrious mountain.

On Chastity

28. I weep as I say that some could not show any less regard for maintaining the vow of chastity. They throw the members of Christ to a harlot, although they well know that he who fornicates in his own body sins and that *no fornicator or covetous person hath inheritance in the kingdom of Christ* (Eph 5:5). Dearest ones, how often we reflect upon those who seem unmindful of salvation, alienated from the truths their lips repeat but thinking baser thoughts than swine wallow-

17. Averbode *vovendo*; Valvekens *vivendo*.

ing in the mud of their slough. These religious *stain and pollute the flesh, and spurn control.*[18]

29. "Not only do they defile their own bodies," one author says, "but they truly despise even the superiors who are endowed with authority over them. They are unafraid to heap curses upon those whom they ought to treat with reverence.

> And yet so great is the perversity of such men, that although they have no cause, nevertheless they curse things they do not understand. Indeed, in direct opposition to the good, they are so corrupted by comfort and lust that—even in matters in which even animals devoid of reason live appropriately and moderately, such as food, drink, and sex—they comport themselves to their own destruction."[19] *These are murmurers, full of complaints, walking according to their own desires, and their mouth speaketh proud things* (Jude 1:16), these who give themselves over to shamelessness, into doing every unclean thing. But you, my brothers, did not learn Christ to be thus. Nevertheless, you have heard and *are awaiting the mercy of our Lord Jesus Christ in eternal life* (Jude 1:21) in himself. Then be merciful toward the others in fear, "hating not the men themselves, but rather this body polluted by earthly affections. For it is as if a filthy garment weighs down and stains the human soul. And this more merciful

---

18. This quotation of Jude 1:8 seems to combine the wording of the Vulgate with the use of *polluunt* as found in Erasmus's New Testament edition: *Novum Testamentum omne, multo quam antehac diligentius ab Erasmo Roterodamo recognitum, emendatum ac translatum* (Basel, 1519), 654.

19. This long quotation is verbatim from Erasmus's *Paraphrase of the Epistle of Jude*. See *Tomus Secundus continens paraphrasim D. Erasmi Roterodami in omnes epistolas apostolicas, etc.* (Basel: Froben, 1532), 351–52. For another English translation of this passage, see *New Testament Scholarship: Paraphrases on Timothy, Titus, Philemon, Peter, James, Jude, John, Hebrews,* ed. Robert Dick Sider, Collected Works of Erasmus 44 (Toronto: University of Toronto Press, 1993), 128–29.

approach is appropriate—to cure strangers who err, for no one living in this body can remain pure.[20]

On Poverty

30. I now speak with trepidation concerning the vow of poverty, since the vice of property in some monasteries creeps so far, blossoms forth, and even extends so far that you may not find even vestiges of true poverty; rather each lives for himself and not his neighbor. From this fact every kind of vice pours forth. The sharing of things in common (*communio rerum*) is uprooted and thrown into disorder. One hungers while another is intoxicated. From this situation arise contentions, jealousy, and complaints; while wealthy members flourish, paupers lack even the bread by which they may drive away hunger. What may I say to you? Do I praise you? No, in this matter I offer no praise. Let those who form this pack pay attention—those who segregate themselves as if they were animals and, carrying off what is meant for all to share, make things their own possessions. Let them pay attention, I say, and before their own eyes place the double dealing of Ananias and Saphira, lest as they are similar to those two in fault, they may also be their equals in punishment.[21]

31. Let them whom it pleases also read Augustine's sermon to the priests of Hippo about the monk Januarius, who in the wall of his cell had one hundred and ten coins (*cyclos*) hidden and laid up until his death—not without grave danger to his soul, as the words of Augustine make clear: "binding the hands of the cadaver, placing his money in the burial cloth and weeping over him, you should say: *Keep thy money to thyself, to perish with thee* [Acts 8:20]. For it is not permitted

---

20. This quotation is verbatim from Erasmus's paraphrase of Jude, 353.
21. See their story in Acts 5:1-11.

to us as servants of God to allow this in the work of the monastery because it is a covenant of damnation."[22] He who has ears to hear, let him understand how grave is the penalty of property that hangs over us. Let him learn to live piously according to the words of his own lips, by which he subjugated himself to the Most High.

32. Christ our Savior, in whose hands have been placed all things that are contained within the bounds of heaven and earth, confesses nevertheless that he has no place where he may rest his own head.[23] We read how the disciples, driven by hunger, broke off ears of grain as they walked across fields.[24] Certainly they left us an example, so we may follow in their footsteps and in the same way cultivate and venerate holy poverty, persisting in the common ownership of things, content to possess clothing and sustenance: *Indeed blessed are the poor, for theirs is the kingdom of heaven* (Matt 5:3).

33. But poverty, you say, is a difficult business. Sometimes it even leads a person overly pressed by penury to blasphemy. But the real cause is meanness of spirit, not poverty. Lazarus was a poor man, exceptionally poor, and his poverty was exacerbated by great sickness. This sickness rendered the poverty itself even more costly, since the severity of his illness begged for many comforts but his poverty could not provide any whatsoever. For indeed either of these ills—sickness or poverty—on its own would

---

22. This version of the story of Januarius is now known to be pseudo-Augustinian. See *Sermo 5 De obedientia ad sacerdotes suos*, PL 40:1245. This medieval work, part of the popular *Sermones ad fratres in eremo*, had been included in the very first printed edition of Augustine's sermons in 1494. See A. Treloar, "The Augustinian *Sermones ad fratres in eremo commorantes*," *Prudentia* 3 (1971): 39–50. For Augustine's authentic discussion of the case of Januarius in Sermons 355 and 356, see Adolar Zumkellner, *Augustine's Ideal of the Religious Life* (New York: Fordham University Press, 1986), 406–22.

23. See Matt 8:20; Luke 9:58.

24. See Mark 2:23.

be grave and sorrowful. But when the two were joined together, it became an intolerable evil for every relief to be withheld. And still more torments were heaped upon Lazarus because he often lay prostrate at the doorway of a rich man who feasted splendidly every day. Surely fancy dishes were placed before Lazarus's very eyes and afflicted the soul of that destitute man more heavily than if he had lived hidden at home,[25] where he would not have gazed upon the gustatory splendors in person. Things that are present, when they are taken away, have more effect[26] than absent things, as the Philosopher demonstrates: "Objects excite[27] possibility."[28] Nor indeed was that cruel rich man softened; rather he privileged himself with luxury and every kind of pleasure. Not even the crumbs from his festive table made their way to Lazarus, yet Lazarus patiently bore all these things, so that just as before he spoke no bitterness or blasphemy to others. When he expired from hunger and cruel suffering, he was repaid more illustriously and splendidly for his patience.[29]

34. These things touch us interiorly, in an allegory, so that we may take up patiently with ready arms the virtue of poverty and flee from the cursed vice of property—living

---

25. Averbode *casa*; Valvekens *casu*.

26. Averbode *monent*; Valvekens corrects to *movent*.

27. Averbode *monent*; Valvekens corrects to *movent*.

28. This saying is regarded by Gabriel Biel (1420–1495), the eminent scholastic theologian and Augustinian canon of Windesheim, as a "commune proverbium." See his *Collectorium sive epitome in magistri sententiarum libros*, published during Panhausen's lifetime in Brixen in 1574, in a modern edition by Wilfridus Werbeck and Udo Hofmann (Tübingen: Mohr and Siebeck, 1977), 4.2, 419. The phrase in its singular form, *obiectum movet potentiam*, is standard in discussions of the faculty of the will. It is found in the works of many medieval thinkers, including Raymond Lull, Duns Scotus, and Thomas Aquinas in *Summa Theologiae*, Ia-IIae, q. 10, a. 2—essentially an application of Aristotle's ideas of motion and causation to the movement of the human will.

29. See Luke 16:19-31, for the story of Lazarus and the cruel rich man.

in common in humility, content with one wardrobe keeper, one cellarer. Any man who is discovered to have acted in a way opposed to this virtue will not evade God as his judge, even if in the present moment God does not punish him but saves that for the gloom of eternal hell. A pauper is made stronger, just as gold is tested in a furnace, by his straitened material circumstances. Hence to him are added crowns and honors. His hunger brought forth an abundance of future goods; his illness brought about eternal life; the sores that the dogs licked carried the splendor of glory though the ministry of angels. You see that not poverty itself, but rather the vice of mean-spiritedness is the real reason we bear poverty unwillingly and with complaint, then fall into the cursed vice of personal property—the seed-bed of every evil in the monastic way of life.

On Obedience

35. But now I would like to say briefly about the virtue of obedience that it has been handed down to us who are established in monasteries that we must observe two things: subjection to the abbot and stability in a place. These must be preserved so that we show ourselves to be so stable that we do not at all think it lowly to be subject to the abbot. From that ideal, however, many stray so very far as neither to yield to their superiors nor to rest their feet in their own monasteries. Rather, whether they reside inside or outside the community, they reproach their own superiors with a biting tongue, surrounding them with hateful speech—now heaping insults to their face, now fabricating a lie behind their back. Sitting in secret, they speak false things and defame their own neighbor, inattentive to what has been written: *The prince of thy people thou shalt not curse* (Exod 22:28; Acts 23:5). And this: *Sitting thou didst speak against thy brother, and didst lay a scandal against thy mother's son; Thou thoughtest*

unjustly that I should be like to thee, but I will reprove thee and set before thy face. Understand these things, you who forget God, lest he snatch you away and there be none to deliver you (Ps 49:20-22). Let them also hear the lawgiver Moses saying, *Your murmuring is not against us, but against the Lord* (Exod 16:8). And let them finally hear that saying of Paul: *Let every soul be subject to higher powers; for there is no power except from God. Therefore he that resisteth the power, resisteth the ordinance of God. And they that resist purchase to themselves damnation.*[30] *Wherefore be subject of necessity, not only for wrath, but also for conscience's sake, for they are the ministers of God* (Rom 13:1-2, 5-6).

The Governance of a Commonwealth is Divided into Three Kinds of Affairs

36. "A commonwealth rests upon order. Therefore we may divide this highest of affairs into three aspects: 1) those that are truly heavenly—in a sense those peculiar to Christ, so everywhere they must be placed before all else; 2) those that are straightforwardly of this world, such as lusts or vices; these must be shunned by all of us; 3) in the middle is a certain type of affair that is in itself neither good nor evil—which Christ has neither sanctioned nor reproved— necessary nevertheless for safeguarding the harmony and state of the whole commonwealth."[31] For the common-wealth should in no way be thrown into confusion. "*Let every human being therefore obey public law, submitting them-selves to magistrates, who whenever punishing evil and elevating*

---

30. Panhausen uses *damnationem* in place of the usual Vulgate *maledictionem*.

31. This quotation is verbatim from Erasmus's paraphrase of chapter 13 of the Epistle to the Romans, 58. For another English translation of the para-phrase of Romans, see Sider, *New Testament Scholarship: Paraphrases on Romans and Galatians*, 73–77.

the good do the business of God. In like manner, *he who resists the magistracy does not resist a human being but God, from whom all authority proceeds. And he who is repugnant to God rightly pays the penalty. Because if we do not wish to be obnoxious to laws or magistrates, let us not think we can achieve this by defiant behavior, but rather by innocence. Let us live rightly, and law is nothing to us.*"[32] But because magistrates and prelates "*administer justice, and God is justice, they are ministers of God, and in a certain way they act as his representatives while applying themselves in the task that is mandated to them by public authority.*"[33] And hear the same herald of grace Paul exhorting Titus with these words: *Admonish them to be subject to princes and powers; to obey at a word and to be ready for every good work* (Titus 3:1). They should not act as ones compelled by fear of punishment, but rather be seen willingly to follow what is honest.

37. Concerning the punishment for disobedience, look to Saul (1 Kgs 15), Jonathan (1 Kgs 14), and Dathan and Abyron (Num 16). If I were to tell about the multitude of those eminent in their royal rank who still were punished and deposed from their thrones on account of the sin of disobedience, I would run out of days rather than examples! If God did not spare them, he will certainly not spare you. *For obedience is better than sacrifices* (1 Kgs 15:22).

On Monastic Silence

38. Now I would like to put these matters aside and say a few things about the virtue of silence, an inestimable treasure as the safeguard of peace and the foundation of religious life.

---

32. Again, see Erasmus's paraphrase of Romans, 58–59.
33. Erasmus, *Epistle to the Romans*, 59.

39. Devout restraint of the tongue and brevity of words—making for reverence and virtue—is the distinguishing support and even highest adornment of religious, and it leads to the most agreeable fellowship of human nature. For by silence peace is nourished and preserved. On the other hand, its neglect easily and necessarily causes every religious virtue to rush headlong into vice. Indeed, when the tongue is loosened, some comments descend into words of malice; careless words about harmless things are perverted to complaints, leading finally toward those curses and lies that sacred literature condemns: *For lying lips are an abomination to the Lord* (Prov 12:22), and detractors are hateful to God. These vices render a soul prone to violent reproaches and curses, and from there it strays into quarrels and contentions. A petulant tongue has this characteristic of vice, that not at all content within its own bounds, it spreads its deadly poison into many other areas and fills all things "with garrulous frogs" (as that one says).[34]

On the Number of Dinner Guests

40. Varro says in his Menippean Satires[35] that a banquet must begin with the number of the graces, then progress to that of the muses—that is, it should begin with three and be able to stop at nine, lest some ill befall the symposium. A smaller number may fall silent, but more may become a noisy uproar. Certain people are always eager to speak but listen to nothing. So we are taught by the divine Scriptures,

34. Presumably a reference to Virgil, *Georgics* 3 v. 431. See *Eclogues. Georgics. Aeneid Books 1–6*, trans. H. Rushton Fairclough (Cambridge, MA: Harvard University Press, 1916), 206–7.

35. This passage is based on a quotation from Varro, whose work survives only in fragmentary quotations, in Gellius's *Attic Nights* 1.11. See Aulus Gellius, *Noctes Atticae*, translated by J. C. Rolfe (Cambridge, MA: Harvard University Press, 2014), 2:436–38.

let every man be quick to hear but slow to speak (Jas 1:19). He who is hasty to speak is not far from the danger of moral lapse, but the gift of silence averts danger. *Hast thou seen,* says the Wise man, *a man hasty to speak? Folly is rather to be looked for, than his amendment* (Prov 29:20).

41. For this reason the pious founders of religious orders—considering the vice of the tongue to hang as a danger over souls—sanctioned and instituted silence, the sober and spare use of the tongue in established times and places, to be observed by all religious with the highest zeal. As ministers directed to the good they established definite punishments against transgressors. For since human nature always tends toward vices, our ancestors considered well that their depraved nature must be coerced by punishments and indeed by the threats of such laws, lest we fall into unseemly habits. Even inside these bounds one who indulges excessively in the vice of talkativeness and desire to speak slips little by little into greater vices. Indeed, it is generally true that we are so shaped by nature that we all become worse when given license, and really should be constrained by the restraints of laws, even punishments, lest we degenerate into behaviors other than those suitable to us.

42. As for guarding against something beforehand, if any one matter was devised and constituted best of all by our fathers, then certainly it might be the religious practice of silence, constraining us in the duty of monastic piety. Indeed, what is the result of the unbroken observation of the remaining things by which we strive by duty toward devotion, such as constant chastity and zeal of continence, cultivation of obedience and poverty, of hymns, prayers, vigils, and the rest of the ceremonies by which God is honored? What, I entreat, does it produce? What of piety do these practices have in themselves? What kind of devout mind is there in all of this, if an incontinent tongue dissipates or even thoroughly obscures and contaminates other endeavors?

43. This vice, in a man's own incontinent flow of words, permits him neither to stand firm in the duties of piety nor to fulfill its tasks. Saint James in his canonical epistle attests this very matter: "Because if among you, I say, anyone seems to himself to be abundantly religious—if he restrains his hand from theft, murder, and the rest of the vices—yet meanwhile does not restrain his tongue from careless words, from detractions, from insults, from base speech in contention, nor restrain his heart from base thoughts, the religion of this man is virtually useless and fruitless."[36] Truly this apostle reminds us particularly to restrain the tongue, for if even a little leeway is allowed to that part of the body, innumerable evils are perpetuated.

44. Oh worst evil of all evils, and indeed most harmful! Take in and admit these things into your heart, indeed all the way into the inner chamber of the heart, most beloved, and do not easily relax the reins on an incontinent tongue. Place a hand over your mouth and check your lip with a finger; humble your souls upon the earth. Otherwise you will hardly evade the decreed penalty. *The yoke and the thong*, says Solomon, *bend a stiff neck, and continual labours bow a slave* (Sir 33:27). And the same man says: *The chief thing for man's life is water and bread, and clothing, and a house to cover shame* (Sir 29:27). These things, that illustrious man says, console the poverty and affliction of heart of the suffering.

45. Understand, I ask, and be wise. Great is the utility of the human tongue,[37] if one uses it for the duty of piety and the true will of God. But perilous indeed is an unrestrained and wanton tongue, especially while the soul is corrupted by depraved desires, hatred, anger, envy, vengeance, and ambition. Just as the fruit draws its taste from its juice, so

---

36. In fact Panhausen quotes from Erasmus's paraphrase of James, 363.
37. Averbode *linguae*; Valvekens *lingua*.

prayer is born of that which is stored in the heart. Just as a good person produces good things from the good treasury of his own heart, so a wicked person bears forth bad things from the wicked treasury of his heart. The hearts of those whom piety and charity fill speak words redolent with the charity and piety stored in the recesses of the heart. But those whose hearts and minds are filled up with envy, pride, greed, anger, and hatred undoubtedly produce prayer and speech reflecting in words the disposition of the heart.

46. Let us therefore take the utmost care so that we do not nourish this serpent, this basilisk in the chamber of our heart—and be wounded by it. Let our heart be pure and devout; then our speech will be pure. *For if your eye will have been pure, the whole body will be full of light* (Matt 6:22). Let us furl in the sails of the tongue, which determine where the course and wind and helmsman are heading. Otherwise foaming waves will rush over the top of the ship, leaving it uncertain in which direction the fates may carry it and where it may be allowed to come to rest. We are immediately subject to a huge danger if we permit the tongue to run entirely wild and vomit forth its own venom. The day will come when our most severe Lord and God will inquire into all our thoughts, words, and deeds, and whatever he will have perceived to be discordant from his own law, he will undoubtedly punish most severely.

47. Meanwhile we miserable little men, overwhelmed by so many vices, falling asleep in each ear,[38] think that we live. Only let it, and this voice will arouse you from sleep:

---

38. This phrase, *in utramque aurem dormitantes*, common in many early modern authors, seems to have originated in the Latin version of the collection of aphorisms of the fifth-century writer Joannes Stobaeus. It was available to Abbot Panhausen in printed editions of the Latin from the 1530s. For a later edition see Hugo Grotius, *Dicta Poetarum quae apud Ioannem Stobaeum exstant* (Paris: Buon, 1626), 98.

Give an account of thy stewardship: for now thou canst be steward no longer (Luke 16:2). And also this: *Go ye cursed into eternal fire* (Matt 25:41). Still you sleep! Will you never arouse yourself? Restrain your tongue and lips from evil so that you do not speak deceit, and you will find rest in your own times. I entreat you, judge in the heart that gospel saying: *Every idle word that men shall speak, they shall render an account for it on the day of judgment* (Matt 12:36). What is a careless word? All fables, all jokes and jests, which are poured forth without benefit for the one talking or the one listening, and accomplish nothing toward eternal salvation.

48. If we must be examined thus concerning a careless word, what must be expected from us about a harsh word, especially if it is bitter and harmful to a brother? Do you believe that after this life the rewards of piety will come to those who have acted well? Do you also think that punishment for impiety will fall upon those who have acted wickedly? No one doubts it. We all hope, and there are some who, with a stricken conscience, fear. What will those men say on that tremendous day of Judgment, I ask, who poured forth the pestilential discourses all their days with their own garrulousness, and equally destroy both the leisure and work of themselves and others? What about those who, in their passion for gossip, exhibit their own venal affairs to all listeners? These certainly will at last descend to the lower parts of hell, *where there shall be wailing and gnashing of teeth* (Luke 13:28).

49. Have you understood all these things? The fisherman finally will feel the bite.[39] In your words, our Savior says, you will be justified and condemned.[40] You will be pronounced just if good words flow and useful words drip

---

39. From Erasmus's *Adages* 1.29. See Erasmus of Rotterdam, *Adagia* (Basel: Froben, 1523), 31.

40. See Matt 12:37.

down from your heart. An evil thought is poisonous only to the one thinking it, but an evil saying pours forth out of the heart of one man and into many more. So the tongue, that wicked and restless member filled with deadly venom—with which we bless God and curse men—must be restrained not only from blasphemy, reviling, quarrels, detractions, and base speech, but from everything, to sum up, that contributes no honest usefulness. For the Lord will judge all these things. Let us therefore place a guard on our mouth lest we sin with our tongue.

Concerning the Five-year Silence of the Disciples of Pythagoras

50. The pagan philosopher Pythagoras bound his disciples to a five-year silence, so that in the meantime they might learn to speak prudently.[41] If a pagan mandated these things, we know how much more we who are said to be religious ought to be obliged to follow these salutary laws, and be confirmed by silence. Those philosophers caused themselves to be silent for an entire five-year period so that they might be able to attain the wisdom of this world. Will we then not restrain our tongue from garrulousness for a small amount of passing time, in order that we may grasp the eternal and true wisdom leading to the heavenly fatherland? I realize that it is hard for a dissolute man to learn discipline, a verbose man to endure silence, a wanderer to remain stable. But it will be much harsher and graver to hear the threats and exceedingly harsh words of the Lord, with the Psalmist saying to a certain man concerning his hasty speech, *All the day long thy tongue hath devised injustice:*

---

41. This tradition goes back to at least Iamblichus, and was repeated by many classical writers. See Iamblichus, *On the Pythagorean Way of Life*, trans. John Dillon and Jackson Hershbell (Atlanta: Scholars Press, 1991), 75.

as a sharp razor, thou hast wrought deceit. Thou hast loved malice more than goodness: and iniquity rather than to speak righteousness (Ps 51:4-5); you preferred worse things for better, false words for true, and embraced injustice more than fairness. *Thou hast loved all the words of ruin* (Ps 51:6), which are accustomed to cast men down headlong in painful ruin, reduce them to nothing.

51. Now that you have heard about the petulance of the tongue, in the same manner you will hear about the poisonous punishment conjoined to this evil. The psalmist says, you will not flee, when perversely you will bear out the sentence of God the Creator of all things, for he will destroy you in the end. He will throw you down as if a poorly put-together house; he will pluck you, just as he will take your soul from the tabernacle of your body; he will punish and erase from the number of the living both you and indeed your progeny, roots and all pulled up.[42] Here do you not see the axe at the root of the trees because of the vice of garrulousness and petulance of tongue? Unless you place a guard on your mouth so that you do not err in your speech, the Lord will pull you up and thoroughly overturn you, destroying you—root and progeny—from the land of the living. Understand these things, you who forget God, lest he seize you and there be none to rescue you.

52. What more does David say, that illustrious divine accompanist? *A man full of tongue shall not be established in the earth: evil shall catch the unjust man unto destruction* (Ps 139:12). An incontinent, garrulous, frivolous, immodest, or even contentious man will not prosper, rather will be turned back and cast down headlong, because he has made his tongue as rough as the serpent's. He has roused it so that it

---

42. See Ps 51:7: *Therefore will God destroy thee for ever: he will pluck thee out, and remove thee from thy dwelling place: and thy root out of the land of the living.*

pours out on others a fatal poison. Indeed, like harmful and pestilential speech, *the venom of asps is under their lips* (Ps 139:4). The psalmist compares pernicious discourse to the poison of an adder, just as harmful and destructive. The illustrious Solomon, beloved of God, noted the vice of the tongue with these words: *As a city that lieth open and is not compassed with walls, so is a man that cannot refrain his own spirit in speaking* (Prov 25:28). *Let us therefore strive to keep our tongues from evil and our lips from speaking deceit. For the silent and wise man shall be honored* (Sir 21:31), *and he that hateth babbling extinguishes evil* (Sir 19:5).

53. Saint Paul, inquiring after the proper way of speaking when necessity demands, clearly describes it for us: *Let no evil speech proceed from your mouth; but that which is good, to the edification of faith, that it may administer grace to the hearers* (Eph 4:29). A wicked tongue shows its pestilence in many ways: it poisons by foul speech, disgraces by disparagement, destroys by accusation, deceives by lying and perjury. So let no evil speech proceed from your mouth. The image of the mind is its speech, its discourse. If we are pure in mind, it does not agree with reason that impure speech will come forth. Nor is it enough that the conversation of a Christian man be harmless, but indeed it ought to be such that in due time, uttered to benefit, it bears fruit for those who hear it. If we do otherwise, we offend not only men by a useless and untimely or harmful conversation, but truly even the Holy Spirit of God who dwells in our hearts.[43] That man is indeed unworthy of the name of monk who does not know how to keep silent. I judge there to be very few mortals who are truly able to refrain from speech; often we

---

43. For the centrality of edifying speech to the vocation of the regular canons, see Caroline Walker Bynum, "The Spirituality of Regular Canons in the Twelfth Century," in *Jesus as Mother: Studies in the Spirituality of the High Middle Ages* (Berkeley: University of California Press, 1982), 22–58.

regret having spoken and not to have kept silence. For sin due to silence may be mended in prayer, "but a word once spoken cannot be retrieved."[44]

54. That man sins less who is immoderately silent than he who is intemperately talkative. For the former vice is not only safer, but indeed more honest. Nothing can be more divine than the wise, well-spoken words uttered in seriousness by one who is wise about this world: "as teachers of speech we have human beings; of being silent, the gods."[45] But the petulant disease of the tongue brings with it a huge and insatiable evil—a desire for gossiping about frivolous matters, especially about the affairs of others having nothing to do either with him who repeats it or with those who are listening. Anyone who is always gossiping can hardly avoid dangerous lapses of the tongue. Telling secrets is useless, dangerous most of all to the one who reveals them, but often too to those among whom they are divulged.

Concerning Moderate and Appropriate Jokes

55. Cheerfulness of speech, along with moderate and well-timed jests, contributes greatly to the joviality of human[46] familiarity, and moderate freedom of speech among friends has a great charm. But these things, when not employed in their own proper place, frequently stray

---

44. Horace, *Epistles* 1.18, 1.71. See Horace, *Satires, Epistles, The Art of Poetry*, trans. H. Rushton Fairclough (Cambridge, MA: Harvard University Press, 2015), 374–75.

45. Plutarch, *De garrulitate* 8. The treatise *On Talkativeness* is found among Plutarch's *Moralia*, available to Panhausen in a Latin edition: Plutarch, *Moralia: De placitis philosophorum*, trans. Gulielmus Beda (Basel: Heruagius, 1531). For a modern edition of the Greek and English translation of this passage, see Plutarch, *Moralia*, 16 vols., trans. W. C. Helmbold (Cambridge, MA: Harvard University Press, 1939), 6:416–17.

46. Averbode *humanae*; Valvekens *humanas*.

into serious danger. In our audience perhaps someone will say, what purpose does the tongue have if it may be allowed to be used so little? But listen patiently, my Pamphilus, and you will understand its use.[47]

56. What end does it serve, then? The tongue was given to men for this purpose—that it be a go-between, so that one person may know the mind and heart of another person. Let it speak the truth with its neighbor, praise the Lord in hymns and with the voices of the sweetly resounding Church. Let it pray in spirit and mind, rejoice in God, speak a psalm to his name. Do you hear the proper use of the tongue? Do these things and you will live.

On Lying

57. But today among Christians—let me not say among religious—how rare is faith in the immortal God! For one thing, many people say one thing but do another. I pass over in silence people who have grown so accustomed to lying that they do not even realize when they are doing it. For what in comedies is considered the behavior of base folk is hardly considered disgraceful among us, who are given the name religious. Among important folk it is actually called prudence. For some lie not only when they attest their religion and their vows in speech, but still more in their false appearance—to the grave ruin of the religious way of life that they insincerely profess. Any deceit is unbecoming to children of the light. Once a lie is perceived, trust is destroyed; with trust removed, all community of

---

47. The rhetorical use of "O Pamphile," employed by Erasmus in several of his Colloquies, ultimately comes from the ancient playwright Terence's *Andria*, line 933. See Terence, *The Woman of Andros. The Self-Tormentor. The Eunuch*, trans. John Barsby (Cambridge, MA: Harvard University Press, 2001), 160–61.

human life is destroyed. For who desires to come to accord with him who is not ashamed to lie? Or who can love one who says nothing from the heart? This evil would be lesser but that the vanity of those lying has made it that one cannot trust those actually speaking the truth. And of course, such men destroy others' confidence in them with their frequent untruthfulness.

58. Nor does this disease come unaccompanied, but it brings with it the pollution of virtues and many other faults. The Lord himself declares this through the mouth of the prophet Hosea, at once speaking to the people of Israel and carrying a threat, proclaiming: *There is no truth and there is no mercy, and there is no knowledge of God in the land. Cursing, and lying, and killing, and theft, and adultery have overflowed, and blood hath touched blood. Therefore shall the land mourn, and everyone that dwelleth in it shall languish* (Hos 4:1-3). The prophet shows that not in vain does an angry God threaten serious penalties and assign punishments and set forth the causes of his indignation. *There is no truth,* he says, *and there is no mercy, and there is no knowledge of God in the land* (Hos 4:1). But on the contrary falsehoods flourish instead of truth, and instead of mercy, cursing, when by quarrels and insults we assail those mistakes of our neighbors that we ought to have healed mercifully and by a secret and fraternal warning.

59. The knowledge of God, however, admits of no contention and acrimony. Rather it is peaceful, modest, compliant, full of mercy and good fruits. In its place instead homicide, theft, and adultery enter secretly—*and blood hath touched blood* (Hos 4:2)—so that sins increase by more sins and old ones are added to new. The prophet points out this abundance of sins when he says *theft, and adultery have overflowed* (Hos 4:2). Who does not know that certainly the greatest sin is when we summon a brother into the danger of crimes of deception?

Concerning the Defilement and Calumny of Another's Reputation

60. But yet more wicked than all these vices is calumny, the attack on and disparagement of the reputation of another. Calumny in the proper sense is vexation of someone in a legal suit through fraud, deception, or artifice, but in metaphor it is understood as false accusation. Hence from the law of the Twelve Tables it is declared, "Let the calumniator suffer the same thing that the accused would, if he had been convicted."[48] *A man that beareth false witness against his neighbor, is like a dart and a sword and a sharp arrow* (Prov 25:18). We fight with dart and arrow from a distance, but by sword at close quarters; the tongue of some is a sharp sword. But it is tedious to pursue all things at length. Anyone may look around and assess quickly how great a pestilence a falsely accusing tongue inflicts.

61. Now when it comes to detraction, how shamelessly we forgive ourselves! Worse, we even flatter ourselves and appear to ourselves as merry and urbane, while we gnaw at the reputation of a brother. God prohibits this in the same place as calumny and detraction when he says, *You shall not lie; neither shall any man deceive his neighbor* (Lev 19:11). *Thou shalt not be a detractor nor a whisperer among the people. Thou shalt not stand against the blood of thy neighbor* (Lev 19:16). For that man beloved to God teaches how detestable an evil detraction is: *The thought of a fool is sin: and the detractor is the abomination of men* (Prov 24:9). He who thinks wickedly about his neighbor even as he curbs his tongue is not immune from sin, but is reckoned harmful only in the eyes of

48. This quotation from the Twelve Tables, the ancient Roman law code, was common in Panhausen's time. See Desiderius Erasmus, *In Laurentii Vallae elegantiarum libros epitome* (Cologne: Gymnicus, 1542), 30.

God. But he who promiscuously wags a poisonous tongue against an absent neighbor is known as abominable and execrable not only to God but even among upright men. This vice is especially common among women, but now has stealthily invested men—most of all the community of religious—and with it flows every sordid and incurable evil of nature.

62. I implore you, most beloved, to purify yourselves from this poison and carefully restrain your tongue from the marketplace of loquacity. Remember that you have two ears and only one mouth, so that you may hear many things and say few things. A certain learned teacher of divine knowledge said, *He that keepeth his mouth, keepeth his soul; but he that hath no guard on his speech shall meet with evils* (Prov 13:3). And the same man said in another place, *He that keepeth his mouth and his tongue, keepeth his soul from distress* (Prov 21:23). *Death and life are in the power of the tongue: they that love it shall eat the fruits thereof* (Prov 18:21).

63. Since these things are acknowledged and held as true without controversy—and everyone agrees that garrulousness of tongue involves great danger—let me just say that almost all evils are simultaneously heaped together in a poisonous tongue. This insanity so twists us that we do not with the prophet *place a guard on our lips* (Ps 140:3) lest we sin by our tongue. How much more should we listen to what our Lord God may say to us with patience and silence? Therefore, lest we transgress the laws of silence, let us be *swift to hear, but slow to speak, and slow to anger* (Jas 1:19).

64. Pious men must distance themselves not only from all vindictiveness, but even from harsh words. Christ, who is *the way, the truth, and the life* (John 14:6), teaches us to speak well about those who curse us, to wish well for those who desire evil things for us. He who looses the restraints of his tongue—a slippery and inconstant member—with

anger and hatred in mind does not pursue these goods. Let our fortitude be placed in hope and silence, lest we prevaricate in speech. *In the multitude of words there shall not want sin; but he that refraineth his lips is most wise* (Prov 10:19). Not only is he prudent who in speaking holds the reins on his tongue, but as Solomon witnesses, *Even a fool, if he will hold his peace, shall be counted wise: and if he close his lips, a man of understanding* (Prov 17:28). From what has been said previously, it is evident that our predecessors were drawn and attracted to that holy ordinance of silence for important, not for trivial, reasons. To be sure, if the tongue were only to be restrained, it would be possible to avoid innumerable evils with ease.

65. In the Book of Job, Eliu speaks with puffed-up cheeks, revealing his desire for too much talk: *for I am full of matter to speak of, and the spirit of my bowels straiteneth me. Behold, my belly is as new wine which wanteth vent, which bursteth the new vessels. I will speak and take breath a little* (Job 32:18-20). Do you hear this man who is so loquacious and impatient of silence? But what did he say before? *I also will answer my part,* he says, *and will shew my knowledge* (Job 32:17). You see here a virulent loquacity joined to a spirit of elation and inane glory, when he says: *I will shew my knowledge.* Woe to that man who offers his own tongue for sale to every passion of the mind!

66. But what does our Savior proclaim instead in the gospel? *I receive not glory from men* (John 5:41), nor do I hunt the human glory that carries with it things dragging us toward eternal death. In your mouth words of no consequence often appear; in your heart ambition for the human praise that opposes sacred eloquence reigns instead. The Lord rebukes certain men, saying, "True piety is to assign the glory of all things to God. How can you believe, when you hold in contempt the glory that is from God alone—while you find

among men the falseness of fawning upon one another yourselves"[49] and embracing the sordid praise of this world? Christ did not seek his own glory; rather his heavenly Father sought it. So for what exactly do you esteem vanity and seek lies, forfeiting eternal life? *God*, as the same one says, *speaketh once, and repeateth not the selfsame thing the second time* (Job 33:14).

67. Certainly he who moderates his discourse is learned and prudent—indeed an erudite man of precious spirit. How eloquently he combines thrift of discourse and the discretion to keep silent when he has no genuine learning! Ecclesiastes recognized *a time to keep silence and a time to speak* (Eccl 3:7). And while a fool shares everything on his mind, a wise man knows to delay and hold back for the next day. As a certain one says, *There is one that holdeth his peace, because he knoweth not what to say: and there is another that holdeth his peace, knowing the proper time. A wise man will hold his peace until he see opportunity: but a babbler, and a fool, will regard no time* (Sir 20:6-7). And: *A parable coming out a fool's mouth shall be rejected: for he doth not speak it in due season* (Sir 20:22).

68. It is a matter of the greatest importance at what time we produce a discourse—before whom, and for which circumstances and situations: *and there is another that is hateful, that is bold in speech* (Sir 20:5). *To speak a word in due time is like apples of gold on beds of silver* (Prov 25:11). Behold how the tradition of our fathers is supported on as firm a defense as possible, including their ordinance about the observation of silence in the determined times and places.

---

49. This quotation is *verbatim* from Erasmus's paraphrase: *Paraphrasis in evangelium secundum Ioannem* (Basel: Frobenius, 1524), 65. The text corresponds with John 5:44.

On the Scarcity of Words of the Spartans

69. Temperance of tongue and brevity of speech have always met with the highest praise not only among Christians but also among the pagans. The Spartans yielded up especially few words. Some people, though, talk constantly; always garrulous and restless, they disturb both the gods and human beings. "An orator of the Corinthians was sent to Sparta. When in the presence of Aegis he had spoken quite extensively; as he wound up his speech he asked if there was something that would have to be reported back to the Corinthians. 'What other thing,' Aegis said, 'except you, having barely been asked to tell in what manner, above all, someone can attain that among men he might have an honest reputation, said "speak those things that are best and do those things that are most honest." What could be said more briefly or what more perfectly?' "[50] Another Spartan, when asked in which manner someone would be able to please men most, responded, "If someone should speak to them pleasant things and then perform useful ones."[51] A certain man, replying to a garrulous barber's repeatedly asking him, "How should I shave you?" answered, "In silence."[52] For he feared that if the garrulous man talked too much, the agitated sawing of the razor might wound him.

70. We have touched upon these things about the vice of loquacity in a few words. For the human spirit entirely to forbid conversation is not fitting, but let it be confined within honest limits, and let such conversation be seasoned by wit. And in place of dishonest facetiousness, arguments,

---

50. Here Panhausen combines two passages from Erasmus: *Apothegmatum libri I–IV*, ed. Tineke L. Ter Meer (Leiderdorp: Brill, 2010), 70, 81.

51. Plutarch, *Sayings of Spartans*, Antalcidas 4; in Plutarch, *Moralia*, 3:301.

52. See Plutarch, *De garrulitate*, chap. 13.

complaints, and verbal abuse, let good conversation be heard offering grace to those listening, so that truly with the prophet we can say, *That which went out of my lips, hath been right in thy sight* (Jer 17:1). Turn again to the heart, secret violators of the law, and attend to the law; *embrace discipline, lest at any time the Lord be angry, and you perish from the just way when his wrath shall be kindled in a short time* (Ps 2:12-13).

71. Therefore stand firm upon your ground—old men and youths, elders, the humblest, and those indeed in the middle ranks—cleansing yourselves from every pollution of the flesh and spirit, completing your sanctification in the fear of God. Purge yourselves, I say, not only from every filth of the body but also of the soul, in order that you may at once live innocently among men and render your spirit acceptable to God. In this way, you prepare a full and perfect sanctity for the time of the coming of Christ while holding yourselves in the duty and fear of that Christ who repays each for his own deeds. Thus, having restrained those things that pertain to either substance, flesh, or spirit, a soul steered by God is the appropriate captain of the body, befitting the dignity of its self-control and giving offense to no one. So you may avoid the censures of critics.

On Pride

72. Furthermore, commit yourselves zealously to the same things to which Christ committed himself—much suffering, daily afflictions, fasting, purity of life, gentleness, authentic rather than purported charity, and truthful conversation. On the one hand, if you are protected by the arms of justice and shielded by an upright conscience, good fortune will not carry you away; on the other hand, adversity will cause you no alarm.

73. But where does the warmth of these words take me? I do not restrain myself from pouring out whatever is in my

heart, for my mouth is open toward you, brothers, and my heart full. Never permit pride in your feelings and in your words to dominate, for all perdition takes its beginning in that very vice. Emend, I beseech you, brothers, emend your ways toward better things when negligently—yet indeed knowingly—you have sinned, lest you seek a space for penance and be unable to find it when you are suddenly seized on the day of death. Let your charity hear the voice of the Lord speaking through the prophet: *Let the wicked forsake his way, and the unjust man his thoughts, and let him return to the Lord and he will have mercy on him* (Isa 55:7); *for he is gracious and merciful and ready to repent of the evil* (Joel 2:13). *For God does not desire the death of the sinner, but rather that he be converted and live* (Ezek 33:11).

74. Turn away then not only from wicked actions but also from wicked thoughts, so that your hands may be innocent and your heart pure—lest beyond that you seem to have received your souls in vain, or that you have acknowledged or given your pledge to your superiors falsely.[53] Rather you should keep laboring in every work of the Lord, knowing that your effort is not empty before God. Let this be your glory, *the testimony of our conscience, that in simplicity of heart and sincerity of God* (2 Cor 1:12), you have been engaged in this world. And when you may anticipate beforehand that your conscience will be pure from all deceit, then you may not despair about God's help. Be eager to show obedience to the magistracy and to your superiors, to possess chastity and purity of soul, to embrace poverty and sobriety. Place a guard and boundary on your mouth, restraining your tongue. Sleep but little, pray often, let sacred readings be on your right and on your left, and meditate on these day and night.

---

53. Averbode *vovisse*; Valvekens *novisse*.

75. Since human affairs are both vile and prone to vanity, we must ascend to a greater life and more excellent dignity, and strive at more complete discipline. Indeed, only through these means does the path lie open to that mind of the Lord. If life seems hard to you, unburden yourself; if difficult, do not regret emptying yourself; if tedious, hurry the more; if laborious, cry out, *Draw me: we will run after thee to the odour of thy ointments* (Song 1:4). Happy is he who runs so that he may grasp, or rather that he may be grasped and led up to the mountain to the vision of the great God, who is above all things blessed forever! Amen.

But now let those who have been listening depart.

Treatise on Monastic Life and Religious Vows

Above all on this account religious life was instituted, and here it drew its origin, to oppose what 1 John 2:16 names: *For all that is in the world is the concupiscence of the flesh, and so forth.*

1. We hold for a certainty that the world is grounded in wickedness—from the statements of the blessed apostle John, from the perception of our own eyes, from what we touch by hand, and from what daily experience most certainly teaches us.[1] Wherever we turn, things offer themselves that lure us away from innocence of life as well as enticing and pushing us towards evil. But let us not *give sleep to* our *eyes or slumber to* our *eyelids, or rest to* our *temples until* we *find out a place for the Lord, a tabernacle for the God of Jacob* (Ps 131:4-5).[2] Let us guard ourselves from disgraceful activities, in the same way that we protect ourselves from death itself. Let us not be slaves to base actions, nor have any dealings with the devil and the world. Whatever tends away from the highest justice is sin, and truly there are many kinds and categories of sin.

---

1. Here Panhausen paraphrases the opening lines of 1 John.
2. The singular pronoun *meis* of the psalmist appears here as *nostris*.

Diverse Kinds of Sins

2. There are capital sins and also venial ones. God forbid that those who once and for all have given up the world and attached themselves to God should be turned again towards a deadly error! And while it may be true that human beings can hardly avoid trivial sins, no fault is so trivial that it should be regarded as of no consequence. For even if a sin seems trivial, nevertheless it is no light thing, even if in comparison with a more serious one it is said to be trivial. In fact, I would venture that even a trivial matter, when undertaken in direct opposition to divine precepts, takes away and drags the soul down to eternal fires. There is nothing trivial in even sight and taste. The father of our race, after he was settled in the sublime seat of Paradise, was thrust down into the depths, affecting himself and his whole posterity disastrously, because he tasted that which had been forbidden. Indeed,[3] Lot's wife was turned into a statue of salt because she gazed back at whence she had come.[4] Therefore we must consider not how great a commandment might be, but rather how great is the one who commands it. So we must understand that no precept must be considered unimportant, however ignored.[5]

For example, effusive, immoderate laughter seems to be a trivial fault. But immoderate laughter slips into mockery, from mockery to detraction, from detraction to violent insults, from insults to more serious things, punished horribly even by human laws.[6] Any type of sin must be shunned

---

3. I read *vero* for Valvekens's *veto*.

4. Gen 19:26.

5. This discussion of the apparent but misleading triviality of some sensual sins is reminiscent of Augustine's discussion of the pear theft in *Confessions* 2.

6. Admonition against immoderate laughter (*risus*) in the monastic context, leading to mockery (*ad scurrilitatem*) can be found in the Rule of Saint Benedict, 4:53-54; 6:8; and 7:59.

by the devout lest, having been treated as of little account, little by little it lead to death. Let us be so insensible to former desires that we may appear dead to them, and let us be committed so that our members, already consecrated to Christ, not thereafter serve the judgment of the devil, the world, and its pomps, so that we do wrong. Rather we should take care to move far beyond all such matters, so that in our entire life it may be transparent that we together with Christ have left behind the things of death and have been brought over to a new life.

A Description of the Wicked World

3. Please tell me, I beseech you, what does this world possess that is not fatal? In which state, in which nation, do you perceive that modesty, honesty, and upright arts still have a place? Do not ambition, crimes, frauds, and deceits seize the rewards of virtue? Listen to Saint John speaking in his canonical epistle. There are three things, he says, by which most of all this world deceives stupid and careless people. *For all that is in the world is the concupiscence of the flesh, and the concupiscence of the eyes, and the pride of life* (1 John 2:16). Certainly, these are the most harmful diseases, sons of perdition,[7] offspring of Satan, children of the ill-starred one. For the world holds out illusions of empty pleasures. From time to time these stroke the senses of the body so that the soul is called away from the pursuit of celestial goods. He who loves the world falls away from the love of the Father.[8] I do not speak here about the world God created, in which we live whether we like it or not, but rather about the dishonest desires for those wicked things in which most people place their happiness.

---

7. See John 17:12; 2 Thess 2:3.
8. See 1 John 2:16.

4. A pure mind rather than a physical location separates us from depraved desires and the world. What good does it do to leave behind the world and inhabit an empty desert, if malice, anger, envy, hatred, pride, and similar feelings still tyrannize us and the human eye inspires greater fear in us than the divine gaze? Nevertheless, for a variety of reasons, we must take note of place.[9] For thus speaks the Lord through the prophet: *Go, my people, enter into thy chambers, shut thy doors upon thee, hide thyself a little for a moment, until the indignation pass away. For behold the Lord will come out of his place, to visit the iniquity of the inhabitants of the earth* (Isa 26:20-21). And again, the Lord speaks in the gospel: *But thou, when thou shalt pray, enter into thy chamber, and having shut the door, pray to thy Father in secret, and thy Father who seeeth in secret will repay thee* (Matt 6:6). He who commands you to pray in secret will reward you. He commands you to pray in secret and in a place separated from those things that might hamper you so that your mind, protected from anxiety about fragile concerns, can be more intent upon the contemplation of celestial things when it addresses the King of heaven and earth with the tongue of a servant.

5. Solitude is always preferable for private prayer. Our Lord proposed himself as an example for us to imitate, when having dismissed the crowd he ascended the mountain to pray alone.[10] For this reason he often removed himself even from his disciples. For he said, *Sit you here, til I go yonder and pray* (Matt 26:36). We also read that he prayed in the town of Gethsemane.[11] Furthermore, in Mark's gospel it is written, *And rising very early, going out, he went into a desert place, and there he prayed* (Mark 1:35). And we are told in Luke, *But*

---

9. Valvekens omits a marginal note in Averbode: *Privatae orationi apta est solitudo* ("Solitude is suitable for private prayer").

10. See Matt 14.

11. Matt 26:36.

at night, going out, he abode in the mount that is called Olivet (Luke 21:37), and spent the whole night in prayer.

6. The path of human life is said to be divided in two directions, between human and divine matters; one way is found among the great throng of people, but solitude pursues the other. David chose to be humbled in the house of his God, rather than to dwell in the tents of sinners.[12] Therefore we must seek a place free from all noisy distraction, if at all possible, for offering prayer to God, so that it may be offered more purely and more sincerely and the incitements of the world be turned away with greater profit. When the human eye has been drawn away from the clouds of this world, our minds are more easily cleared of images of transient things. When the good and prudent man has put such things aside, he offers his whole self to God in the total submission of service.

The Origin of Monks

7. Drawn by this conviction, some persons of both sexes, beloved followers of God,[13] inflamed by faith and zeal for devotion, have left behind the world with its own desires, empty show, and fallacious delights. Rejecting the scab and filth of habits and worldly needs, they removed themselves to deserts and secret places, the vast wastes among the woods and sands. For this reason they were called monks or solitaries. They took their model from Christ and his disciples. Concerning the practice of the poverty of Christ, they recalled to mind his counsel: *And every one that has left house, or brethren, or sisters, or father, or mother, or wife, or children, or lands for my name's sake, shall receive an hundredfold, and shall possess life everlasting* (Matt 19:29). And in another passage, *Hearken, o daughter, and see, and incline thy ear, and*

---

12. See Ps 83:11.
13. Averbode *homines Deo amabiles*; Valvekens *hominem Deo amabilem*.

forget thy people and thy father's house. And the king shall greatly desire thy beauty (Ps 44:11-12).

8. To live in the secular world would be praiseworthy if it were a place where justice, devotion, faith, religion, chastity, continence, generosity, fortitude, and virtues took the lead everywhere. But in reality, since shadows fall all around and the multitude of vices dominates far and near, not only did these people prudently seek what is best, but they also banished the wicked and deplorable things close at hand. The monastic way of life precedes all the other orders except for priesthood. The necessity to flee the cruelty of unbelievers first gave rise to this way of life among Christians, but soon its advantage and delight made it well known. For nothing is sweeter to a pure soul than contemplation, and solitude is the companion, or better yet nursemaid of contemplation.

9. Ancient philosophers deemed a man wise to whom it was permitted to ground his whole life in contemplation. So our forefathers, zealously seeking Christian devotion, left behind those things of the world and went into the groves and among the caves of wild animals and so lived their lives. They did so that they might be more free for contemplation, with no one interrupting, reckoning that among the multitudes and company of men, they would be less able to find God. For many things in the world impede this pursuit—many things call us back from a holy purpose—for we see or hear many things that begin to stimulate the senses to the hope of a dishonest desire. When men become genuine solitaries, they pass over human matters in silence, seeing or hearing none of those things that are happening in the secular world. Their souls enjoy an undisturbed peace drawing them toward the crucified Lord of majesty, the image of whom they put on when they show themselves stripped bare[14] and dead to the world.

---

14. Averbode *nudos*; Valvekens *nundos*.

10. When it comes to those things that concern the senses, every occasion of sin has been taken away. They do not gaze upon women, do not handle money, do not engage in legal suits; insults are not heard among them; they do not buy, sell, invest, make contracts, exchange money. In short, no one causes any trouble for them, nor do they trouble others. No struggle would remain for them except that monks are troubled by base thoughts aroused by demons. Nevertheless, their battle goes on against those baleful and hostile enemies so that they may lead a righteous triumph into their homeland. Their enemy must be scorned rather than dreaded, because all his power is in persuasion, and he cannot overcome anyone except one who first is willing. Therefore we must be vigilant and sharply resist the depraved suggestions of demons, for they assiduously wander about and test every opportunity to corrupt, to make evil servants out of good ones and wicked ones even worse.

11. And yet I would not deny that when someone shines forth in greater virtues, the devil attacks and assaults him more sharply. For that reason he beset Adam in Paradise, because of how great his dignity was. Let those attend to these things who in their loftiness excel others in dignity. Yet in this struggle undertaken against so great a beast, we have God's protection. Indeed, after the whole war has ended, God is content that we for our part have brought forward into the fight some zeal and labor, so he may offer us suitable rewards, just as if our own labors had brought the whole conflict to an end. God wishes us to fight back against the devil, with a resolute and watchful mind, for his honor and our salvation. He then in turn will cast him out and put him to flight, and at the last summon us, as it were vigorous soldiers, to our reward, just as he always showed mercy with our fathers.[15] He will never cease to do so.

---

15. See Luke 1:54-55. The passage resonates with the *Magnificat*, sung every evening as part of Vespers.

12. In these ranks have been devout monks, chaste virgins, and the select rank of anchorites, all of whom embraced the monastic life, who voluntarily bound themselves by the vows of chastity, poverty, and obedience and with the grace of God zealously attempted to repay to the Lord God the vows their lips had spoken. I make no empty judgment of these people. Indeed, we may recall from the epistle of John mentioned previously[16] that three pollutions stain this world. In place of desire and pleasure of the flesh, the monastics clearly embraced the splendid virtue of chastity; instead of desire of the eyes and lust for passing things, voluntary poverty; in place of pride or haughtiness of life, humble and prompt obedience. He who preserves chastity of mind and purity of body is a distant stranger to the vice of fornication and of flattery and of the remaining desires of the flesh. That man is truly chaste who always embraces voluntary poverty, is content with his food and clothing, and does not pant after the property of a neighbor, or a wife, or children, or a family, or any of these sorts of things. This man has no commerce with greed and no business with desire of the eyes, which grows like avarice from the desire for many things.

13. He who is humble of heart obeys the commands and dictates of superiors, shows himself docile to all, spurns no one, and out of fairness esteems all. Such a one has for a long time now made a complete divorce from the wickedness of pride, and must be considered truly obedient. He will be permitted to gaze upon the face of the primitive church, to contemplate those first athletes competing in the context for the prize and crown of eternal life.[17] But this struggle is not carnal, nor is it fought with carnal arms, but rather with

16. 1 John 2:16.
17. See 2 Tim 4:7-8.

spiritual ones. Thus Saint Paul says, *For though we walk in the flesh, we do not war according to the flesh, for the weapons of our warfare are not carnal but mighty to God, unto the pulling down of fortifications, destroying counsels, and every height that raises itself against the knowledge of God* (2 Cor 10:3-4). He says, as it were, bound in mortal flesh; nevertheless we do not serve as soldiers under the command of the flesh, but rather in the garrison of the Spirit and of God. Nor are we unarmed, for we have the strength to defeat these enemies—the devil, the flesh, and the secular world, avarice, luxury, and pride of life. The weapons of this warfare, which is spiritual, are not of a human sort, of iron or strong steel. They come instead from the power of God inspired in us to demolish whatever adverse things befall. We cast these down and overturn their cunning strategies, all tools and armaments, not on our own but by the virtue and power of God.

14. The throng of these religious, strengthened in the Lord God by the badges of their virtues, are then fortified by the power of his virtue, just as a strong soldier *puts on the breastplate of faith* (1 Thess 5:8) and *armor of God* (Eph 6:13), and indeed quickly *as a giant to run the way* (Ps 18:6) of the commandments of God. He takes with himself most faithful handmaidens for his journey, that is fasting and prayer, and lest anything be lacking, *princes went before joined with singers in the midst of young damsels playing on timbrels* (Ps 67:26), who embellish this loveliness[18] and by their own presence render it splendid. Thus all things are accomplished in the power of the virtue of God, chastely and with gladness of heart. The princes and timpanists appear to signify this to us. *For God loveth a cheerful giver* (2 Cor 9:7). Fasting and prayer are necessary *against the rulers of the world, of this darkness, and against the spirits of wickedness in the high places*

---

18. Averbode *hoc*; Valvekens *non*.

(Eph 6:12). *This kind is not cast out but by prayer and fasting* (Matt 17:20).

15. With these demons we must struggle continually day and night. Is it not true that that utmost champion of this world, *the devil, as a roaring lion, goeth about seeking whom he may devour* (1 Pet 5:8); he *hath made ready his arrows for them that burn* (Ps 7:14), so that he may strike the righteous in the secret chamber of their heart. We should not be frightened by the deceits of that one himself, *of the arrow that flieth in the day, of the business that walketh about in the dark: of invasion, or of the noonday devil* (Ps 90:6), if we place all our hope and trust in God. For he is the one who on the altar of the cross cast down all the power of Satan. He is our refuge and strength, our help in tribulations. He will strike to the ground all this shadowy army—not only enemies we may see but even those who are unseen, both by day and by night. And he will blunt and break their bow, shield, and sword.

The Deceits and Frauds of Satan and the World

16. But now let us move on to the artifice, frauds, and weapons of Satan and this world. For he is endlessly artful, and he is not easily imprisoned. Satan has his own spirit, through which[19] he supplies a pernicious love of things. There is no reward for those who devote themselves to this world. He prompts desires for foods and drinks to tempt the throat and palate. Let me pass over in silence how the mind grows sluggish in sweet rest and sleep. I make no mention here of shameless fables, by which he flatters the ears, or the various spectacles by which the eye whiles away the time. Everywhere he calls the minds of men from true and eternal goods to empty images. As for that man who is

---

19. Averbode *quem*; Valvekens *quam*.

captured by desire for these things, let him know that he is not roused by the spirit of the heavenly Father, but rather by the spirit of the devil and this world of vanity, beyond all dispute grounded in evil. Whoever loves the world falls away from the love of God the Father, since all that is in the world is desire of the flesh and eyes and pride of life, which is not from the Father, but from the world.

Concerning the Three Desires of the World

17. These three desires and lusts of the world bring great annoyance to those pursuing the monastic life. The desire of the flesh, which by a foolish and filthy itch titillates the members of the body, often prompts the evils of sexual appetite. It also prompts desire of the eyes—the poison of avarice, the ostentation of goods, the clanging of riches and incitements of ambition by which the hearts of men are drawn along to every illicit thing. In addition, it prompts us to covet high status and pride of life, the mother and root of all evils—the most harmful disease for humankind and the murderous betrayal of eternal salvation. But here an army of virtues labors hard and itself *sets up a wall for the house of Israel in the Day of the Lord* (Ezek 13:5). This war between the world and those who gird themselves tightly by monastic vows—most important, chastity of mind and body, voluntary poverty, and humble obedience—is perpetual.

18. That conflict, or better yet, war—for so the ancients called it, fought by two sides contending for victory—is arduous and heavy. On both of the two sides in this struggle are three ranks of virtues and vices. Their threefold battle line is broken only with difficulty. And if any individual prevails against the first line, two others remain against him. But the soul must not be cast down on account of this annoyance. Rather it must recall to mind how our fathers faced the endless prospect of death but nevertheless victoriously

prevailed against their enemies. In them our own affairs are presaged, so we should follow in their footsteps in order that we may know the kindness of God just as they did in their struggle.

19. Just as there is one God of all, he contributes various favors to all and extends mercy to those beseeching him. *For the Lord God knoweth how to deliver the godly from temptation* (2 Pet 2:9), for he is faithful. Nor will he allow us to slip away so far to the point that we may be overcome by the evils besetting us. Truly, even if he suffers some evil to befall us, he will so temper the outcome that we can endure. David, both king and prophet, confirms this: *When I was in distress, thou hast enlarged my heart* (Ps 4:2), that is, you brought me consolation greater than my pain.

20. Therefore let us say, *The Lord is my helper, and I will look over my enemies* (Ps 117:7). If we have[20] the Lord of the universe as our support, the onslaught of the enemy must not make us afraid, but having obtained aid from him we will see the slaughter of the enemy forthwith. Therefore these virtues are called "evangelical counsels"—in that on account of their excellence, the Lord counsels more than commands them. And at the least[21] they strive toward this, that a soul thoroughly stripped of a disordered love of temporal things offers its whole self to God, and by contemplating that highest good with pure eyes it may be zealous to fulfill the will of God through all things. Let it be paramount, then, that those who have bound themselves by these vows always hold in readiness the weapons best suited for every assault of the devil. With these they may break the assault or turn aside the spears of the attacking enemy.

---

20. Valvekens omits *habemus.*
21. Averbode *nimirum*; Valvekens *minime.*

Concerning Faith and its Armor

21. First and most important, we must have the shield of faith, by which religious may defend themselves so that they fully trust God's promises and firmly believe that whatever God has promised, he is able to do. With this shield they ward off whatever frightful things befall. Whatever burning darts—that is carnal desires—that cunning enemy hurls at them, they repel with the bow of chastity. And they wield chastity in opposition to concupiscence of the flesh, allowing no spear of Satan to penetrate their entrails. Let them gird the loins of the soul, by which they always stand erect and unmoving, holding lamps burning in their hands, so that when the Lord comes he will find them watching.[22]

The Meaning of Lamps in Hands

22. The lamps burning in their hands are works of justice, the foundation of which the Lord desired to be chastity, while the loins with their power of generation ought first to be restrained by the belt of chastity. And if contempt of empty and fleeting things is added to chastity, this then is voluntary poverty. We must fear nothing in desires of the eyes or the vice of avarice, for when we have a pure state of mind these matters cause nothing but annoyance. And so *truth will encompass* them *with the shield* of poverty, *so that* they *will not be afraid of the terror of the night, and of the business that walketh about in the dark* (see Ps 90:5-6). But the Lord their protector will quickly drive away all adversaries, and will make specters fear lest

---

22. See Luke 12:35-36. This image of religious, and specifically Premonstratensian canons, as lamps burning in a dark place, echoes the words of Anselm of Havelberg in *Epistola apologetica,* PL 188:188a. See Caroline Bynum, "The Spirituality of Regular Canons in the Twelfth Century," in *Jesus as Mother: Studies in the Spirituality of the High Middle Ages* (Berkeley: University of California Press, 1982), 40.

evil approach them and the scourge approach their tents. At last if pride of life will attack, and will desire to place its own throne among them, humble obedience will protect them at each attack of the spears and so repel adversaries. *He will brandish his sword; he hath bent his bow* (Ps 7:13) and will protect them, lest every injustice dominate them.

23. Within religious communities continuous war is waged against these adversaries, namely desire of the flesh and of the eyes and pride of life. By the arms of obedience, chastity, and voluntary poverty, religious protect themselves and even conquer, not at all indeed by their own strength, but with the aid of Christ their general, under whose command this war is waged. As the words of the Apostle confirm, *neither he that planteth is anything, nor he that watereth, but God that giveth the increase* (1 Cor 3:7).

The Threefold Division of Temporal Things

24. Worldly matters often lead us away from the love and contemplation of God. Some, like riches, are partly outside us, partly joined to us. Likewise, there are those things that have been conjoined to us, as though connected by nature or relation—such as parents, neighbors, or relatives. Other things, though, are entirely within ourselves, such as our own will, and these still more can separate us from God. Therefore, first of all our Savior advises that we relinquish these exterior things on account of the good of conscience and perfection of divine charity.

Whence the Three Vows Have their Origin, and on What they are Founded

25. The vow of poverty is founded upon this counsel, where Christ says, *If thou wilt be perfect, go sell what thou hast and give to the poor, and thou shalt have treasure in heaven, and come follow me* (Matt 19:21). The second counsel, namely

obedience or the relinquishment of one's own will, is founded in the Gospel, where it is written, *If any man come after me, let him take up his own cross and follow me* (see Luke 9:23). And the third counsel, which is chastity, has its foundation in the eighteenth chapter of Luke's gospel, where you may read, *There is no man that hath left house or parents or brethren or wife or children, for the kingdom of God's sake, who shall not receive much more in this present time, and in the world to come life everlasting* (Luke 18:29-30). And again: *If any man come to me, and hate not his father and mother and wife and children, he cannot be my disciple* (Luke 14:26). More will be said below about eunuchs.[23] And so in these words is founded the vow of perpetual chastity.

26. Through these vows all the company of regular religious abandon themselves and all things, so that they subsequently display their own members, now consecrated to Christ to fight for God rather than serve the devil in vices. Nor should they now serve as soldiers under the command of the devil to achieve wickedness, which is death-bearing, but now must betake themselves to new pursuits. They are held up before all others, for their life is exemplary in their having abandoned all to Christ. It is just that we serve under him completely. When once we have offered our names and have been uniformed in his white garment, we rightly have no commerce at all with the Devil. These things now we abandon, shaking off their yoke, and emerge to offer ourselves to God in perpetual sacrifice.

Concerning What Constitutes Christian Liberty; Concerning a Vow

27. Some hold wickedly that those who inscribe themselves in the monastic life also bind themselves perpetually

---

23. Presumably a reference to Matt 19:12.

by the bonds of vows in a manner contrary to Christian liberty.[24] But these people have eyes and do not see, ears and do not hear,[25] and dark is their foolish heart. Believing themselves to be wise, they have been made foolish. Listen, my brother in the Lord, I beseech you, listen. Christian liberty in this most of all consists—that a person can either keep a vow or not. For his own judgment has decided whether he wished or did not wish to make a vow. God does not command a vow to be made, but rather to be fulfilled (Ps 75:12). Indeed, a marriage not yet contracted is not binding. However, when once it is contracted it is firm and insoluble, and so binding that it cannot be dissolved without canonical process. And so it is with the vows of religious. When someone voluntarily, with deliberate intentionality, speaks and confirms a vow by oath, if he does not keep it, the Lord God demands it from the hands of that person himself. For so we read in Deuteronomy: *When thou hast made a vow to the Lord thy God, thou shalt not delay to pay it; because the Lord thy God will require it. And if thou delay, it shall be reputed to you as a sin* (Deut 23:21).

28. If you do not wish to promise, you will be without sin. But you will observe what your lips promised to the Lord your God, and what you have spoken by your own will and with your own mouth. That faithful servant of the Lord going out and coming in says thus in his verses: *Vow ye and pay it to the Lord your God* (Ps 75:12). And further: *It is much better not to vow, than after a vow not to perform the things promised. . . . for an unfaithful and foolish promise displeases him* (Eccl 5:3-4). Also in the Book of Numbers we read, *If any man make a vow to the Lord, or bind himself by an oath, he shall not make himself void, but shall fulfill all that he promised* (Num

---

24. Clearly a reference to Lutheran criticisms of monastic vows.
25. See Ps 113:13; Jer 5:21; Ezek 12:2.

30:3-4). And similarly, for a woman: *Whatsoever she promised and swore, she shall fulfill in deed* (Num 30:5). For this purpose, the prophet Jonah cries out to God, *But I with the voice of praise will sacrifice to thee; I will pay whatsoever I have vowed for my salvation to the Lord* (Jonah 2:10).

29. Clearly, then, a vow does not stand against Christian liberty, but rather is its defense and protection. That is what Scripture teaches, nature dictates, and honor commands. Indeed, vows do compel ordinary servitude, but servitude to Christ, and this servitude is the highest liberty. For that reason the Apostle says, *Being then freed from sin, we have been made servants of justice* (Rom 6:18) and God. And further: *Know you that to whom you yield yourselves servants to obey, his servants you are whom you obey, whether it be of sin unto death, or of obedience unto justice* (Rom 6:16).

30. Therefore none can doubt that chastity, poverty, and humble obedience, according to numerous passages from the Scriptures, are pleasing to God. Who, unless weak of mind and deprived of common sense, does not embrace these virtues with both arms? The one who seeks after false light in the middle of a clear day is absurdly misled.[26] Those who do so are withered branches on the tree, diseased members in the body, a bear in the vineyard, a snake in the field, a wolf among sheep.

Concerning Verbal Abuses of Religious

31. Indeed, the most miserable enemies of all—both men of peace and also perpetual enemies of peace—reproach the habits and abuses of religious. But here I do not wish to take up a defense, since not only do they alone destroy peace but even old men and young do, princes and peasants, rich and

---

26. Averbode *dementiae*; Valvekens *clementiae*. Averbode *commentitie*; Valvekens *commentitiae*.

poor alike. All are spattered by these stains. Their disease has wrought impiety and spreads it everywhere.[27] Nor let any religious think to seek after that justice that is from God by rule, profession, vestment, ceremonies, or variety of habit, or to place the end of salvation chiefly in these things. They least of all, no! For they are not so stupid, so bloated and paunchy, that they cannot tell black from white. We acknowledge justice in mankind as twofold—as also our first fathers, anchorites and monks, acknowledged, who more than a thousand years previously led the monastic life with honor. But we attribute the justice we embrace through faith to Christ Jesus alone. Saint Paul says of this, *that I may be found in him not having my justice, which is of the law, but that which is of the faith of Christ Jesus, which is of God* (Phil 3:9).

32. From these words[28] it follows that justice, which flowed out of the precious blood and passion of Christ,[29] is what saves and justifies us. *For there is no other name under heaven given to men, whereby we must be saved* (Acts 4:12). *That voice of rejoicing in the tents of the just* (Ps 117:15). *Behold the Lamb of God, behold him who taketh away the sin of the world* (John 1:29).

33. But that other justice, which we call human, this both God and Scripture demand from us—not to commit theft, not to commit adultery, and the rest of the things covered in the Decalogue. These, apart from faith, do not justify a person by themselves. But he who will have done these things[30] will live in them; that is, he will evade the punishments that must befall transgressors. No one, however much he may be justified, should understand himself to be free from the observance of the commandments. When he

---

27. Averbode *imperium*; Valvekens *impium*.
28. Valvekens omits *verbis*.
29. Averbode *Christi*; Valvekens *Christo*.
30. Averbode *haec*; Valvekens *hoc*.

is justified and made a friend of God, he is renewed in *advancing from strength day by day* (Ps 83:8); as the Apostle says, that is, by *mortifying the members* (Col 4:5) of his own flesh and displaying those weapons toward sanctification through the observance of the commandments of God, he grows and is more justified. *He that is righteous*, says the Scripture, *let him be made righteous still* (Rev 22:11). And again, *be not afraid to be justified even to death* (Sir 18:22); and further, *Do you see that by works a man is justified, and not by faith only* (Jas 2:24)?[31]

34. We must follow the naked Christ, treating the contemptible delights of the world like manure. But how? Listen to Saint Paul: *that denying ungodliness and worldly desires, we should live soberly and justly and godly in this world, looking for the blessed hope and coming of the glory of [the Great God] our Savior Jesus Christ* (Titus 2:12-13). To this is added chastisement of the body, fasting, and abstinence from the food and drink that reduce the flesh to servitude and deceive the spirit. Does it not seem to you that such things may be able to be fulfilled in monasteries with greater advantage and benefit than in the great and spacious ocean of this world, where *there are creeping things without number* (Ps 103:25)? Hence Saint Bernard says, "In monastic life he falls more rarely, and rises more easily."[32]

31. Much of this paragraph is a close paraphrase of Council of Trent, Session 6, Decree on Justification, Chapter 10 (1547). For the text, see Norman Tanner, ed., *Decrees of the Ecumenical Councils* (London: Sheed & Ward; Washington, DC: Georgetown University Press, 1990), 2:675.

32. This final quotation from Saint Bernard, as well as Panhausen's various scriptural quotations and the discussions of the various meanings of *iustitia*, are simplified presentations of those found in Conradus Klingius, "Loci communes theologici pro ecclesia catholica," in *De monachatu religiosorum* (Cologne: Birkmann, 1559), 223–24, chap. 62. The same is true for Panhausen's discussion of "Christian Liberty," pars. 28–29 above.

On the Different Orders and Clothing in Religious Life

35. Again, let not the mockery of critics disturb you when they point out that among monasteries there may be distinction in pattern of life, diverse rules, and the use of different colored vestments. For cowls and clothes do not make a monk, but rather a pure mind and spotless life. So let it be the case that rule, order, or vestment may be varied but that still there be unity of mind, above all that there be *one heart and one soul on the way to God.*[33] Those men recognize, cultivate, invoke, and honor this—those who are clothed in white, in black, or in any other color or mantle. They possess one faith, one hope in God, and they love him with their whole heart, with their whole soul, and with all their strength.[34] They esteem neighbor with sincere[35] affection, and they joyfully offer others what they wish to be done to themselves. They eat together, they drink together, from one closet they are clothed, by night and by day their prayers are in common. No one says that anything is his own.[36]

36. Yet they are forced by those who hate peace to hear the reproaches of critics whose mouths utter arrogance. In this our own time, all the ministers of Satan laud the fact that the households and servants of secular lords sport the conspicuous weight of boots and clothes spotted and decorated by diverse colors continuously flowing down to the ankles—more like panthers than human beings.[37] Add to this their tailoring of clothing with great waste of cloth. Blind eyes pass over this, or else it is praised by all, and everyone considers it becoming. The clothing of monks

---

33. *Rule of St Augustine* 1.2.
34. See Mark 12:30.
35. Averbode *syncero*; Valvekens *syncere*.
36. *Rule of St Augustine* 1.3.
37. *vestesque diversis coloribus variatas atque depictas, pardis magis quam hominibus similes deserant.* Valvekens omits the second half of this sentence.

alone is deemed a sin. Say, I beg you, since far and wide secular men parade about with clothes so extravagant as to make demons shudder, why is it not allowed for a monk—on behalf of the ancient observance and custom of his order—to be free to wear lowly and abject clothes as signs of penance? In the Old Law, men were accustomed to placate God by sackcloth and ashes. See 1 Kings 10 & 24; 2 Kings 19; Nehemiah 9; Esther 4; Job 16; Psalm 29; Isaiah 15 & 58; Joel 1; Jonah 3. Here we read of sackcloth. What are monastic vestments other than a form of sackcloth, which the ancients wore long ago in the season of penance? Let those who seek dissension among us then let it be. We might say the same thing about the practices and the verbal assaults of judges.

37. Some weak-minded men judge monastic vows to be impossible, beyond fulfillment by any religious. I would believe the like also if religious were held up by human strength only and not by the cooperation of divine grace. *For it is God who worketh in* us, *both to will and to accomplish* (Phil 2:13).[38] It is Paul himself, the faithful athlete of Christ, who says, *But by the grace of God I am what I am. And his grace in me has not been void; but I have labored more abundantly than all they. Yet not I, but the grace of God with me* (1 Cor 15:10).

38. The same apostle confesses that he can do all things through him who strengthens him.[39] *And God is faithful*, if in him we place all our trust, *who will not suffer you to be tempted above that which you are able* (1 Cor 10:13). Let us not despair that he who has given us desire will grant that it be fulfilled in Christ Jesus.[40] What if it is true that certain lax religious have not attained the goal and perfection of monastic life? Must we therefore be dismayed? No indeed! Is it not better

38. Panhausen shifts from *you* to *us*.
39. See Phil 4:13.
40. See Phil 1:6; 2:13.

to persevere in things well begun? I am kept from praising this sentiment. As for him who has fallen, does it not behoove him to rise again? Most of all! For he will stand: God has the power to set his servant up and strengthen him lest he falter. But now let our study return to the evangelical counsels and the way of life of regular religious.

On the Vow of Chastity

39. Saint Paul says, *Now concerning virgins, I have no commandment of the Lord; but I give counsel, as having obtained mercy of the Lord, to be faithful. I think therefore that this is good for the present necessity* (1 Cor 7:25-26) and the difficulties that stem from marriage or the evils of marriage. Concupiscence of the flesh and engagement in sexual love greatly impede the exercise of reason—absorb and reduce it as if to nothing. The conjugal bond, although licit, implicates a person in the many cares and desires of the world, as the Apostle attests: *He that is without a wife is solicitous for the things that belong to the Lord: how he may please God. But he that is with a wife is solicitous for the things of the world, how he may please his wife, and he is divided* (1 Cor 7:32-33). That is to say that he is separated from the benefit and advantage of virginity, making it as difficult as possible to adhere to God with a whole and free mind. Perpetual chastity is a lofty matter, undertaken as a commission of Christ. Therefore it is by Christ that those who voluntarily embrace the virtue of chastity on account of the kingdom of heaven are lifted up with the highest honors.

40. The gospel text is a witness to this teaching. When the Lord concluded his discussion with the Pharisees about divorce between a man and a woman, he charged, *What therefore God hath joined together, let no man put asunder* (Matt 19:6). The disciples, considering this a grave and burdensome teaching, interposed their different opinion in these

words: *If the case of a man with his wife be so, it is not expedient to marry.* Jesus responded to them, *All men take not this word, but they to whom it is given* (Matt 19:10-11). Furthermore, that he might show that the celestial kingdom is the inheritance of the chaste, he adds, *there are eunuchs who have castrated themselves because of the kingdom of God* (Matt 19:12) and offered themselves as eunuchs voluntarily, to quote Tertullian.[41] That is, those who have turned the freedom to marry to the purpose of chastity, by which more purely and more freely they might serve God and be companions to the angels in heaven as having lived the angelic life on earth. About them it has been said, *for they shall neither marry nor be married, but shall be as the angels of God in heaven* (Matt 22:30). This is a spiritual castration, grounded in an individual's liberty. No one is compelled to do this unwillingly, only one who voluntarily binds himself by a vow. Saint Paul leaves this in the judgment of each person, so that each may discern concerning this matter what he should decide.[42]

41. Indeed, marriage may be chaste and the marriage bed without stain, while virginity may be impure. The Apostle praises celibacy as the happier state, but he approves matrimony as safer. He compels no one, nor does he prohibit, at least in those matters in which the Lord does not compel or prohibit. He confesses about virgins that he has no command, but he gives advice how to obtain mercy from God as a person of faith. He distributes to others those things he has obtained by the grace of God so that he may be a giver of counsel and a faithful minister.

42. The habits of our bodies and indeed of our minds are mutually dissimilar. The same advice cannot be given to everyone, but it is necessary that each reflect on his own strength regarding the type of life to which by nature he is best fitted,

41. See Tertullian, *Liber de Monogamia* 5, PL 2:936A.
42. Averbode *viderit*; Valvekens *viderat*.

then embrace it. Paul compels no one to marriage, nor prohibits marriage, but leaves what is suitable to be weighed
carefully by the soul of each one, nevertheless judging an
individual happier if he perseveres according to the advice
Paul has given. Saint Ambrose responds beautifully to the
Apostle in chapter 3 of the first epistle to Timothy, where he
writes, "A good wife is rightly praised, but a devout virgin is
still preferred, as the Apostle says: *Therefore, both he that giveth
his virgin in marriage, doth well; and he that giveth her not, doth
better* (1 Cor 7:38). The latter thinks of the things that are of
God, the former of those things that are of the world. The first
is bound by conjugal bonds, the second is free of them. The
one is under law, the other under grace; care increases through
a woman, but safety comes from a virgin."[43]

43. Chastity then requires that a person be zealous to live
uncorrupted, by means of deliberate and constant counsel,
from every stain of the flesh or sexual pleasure, and to lead
a celibate life continently that he may be holy in body and
spirit on account of Christ. Regarding this the Apostle
spoke: *for he that hath determined, being steadfast in his heart,
having no necessity, but having power of his own will; and hath
judged this in his own heart, to keep his virgin, doth well* (1 Cor
7:37)—and rightly so. Just as it is not safe then to hinder one
who wants to from marrying, so it is impious to dissuade
someone from the pursuit and vow of chastity. *The time is
short. It remaineth that they also who have wives be as if they had
none . . . and they that use this world, as if they used it not; for
the fashion of this world passeth away* (1 Cor 7:29, 31).

44. Let concern for heavenly things come first, and only
afterwards make use of things such as the mundane business dealings and legal cases in which necessity involves

---

43. Ambrose, Epistle 42, PL 16:1124C. This passage is cited in Thomas
Campegius, *De coelibatu sacerdotu non abrogando* (Venice, 1554), sec. 11.

us, just as if we are not using them. To blurt about the trou-blesomeness[44] of women, by which almost all pages of the Scriptures are stained, has no use unless to bring up that single remedy Solomon acknowledges: *And I have found a woman more bitter than death, who is the hunter's snare, and her heart is a net, and her hands are bands. He that pleaseth God shall escape from her: but he that is a sinner, shall be caught by her* (Eccl 7:27). *One man among a thousand I have found, a woman among them all I have not found* (Eccl 7:29).

45. This world contains shadows of good and evil things in which there is nothing solid or long-lasting, to which those who tend towards immortality may cling with all their mind. The height of being seriously Christian is that, having denied impiety and secular desires, we live soberly and piously in this world, resisting all manner of baseness and vices, all impurity of life, and reach out with our entire selves toward God. With the innocence of true Christians, we walk without stain in the way of the Lord as chaste and modest virgins.

46. We read in Isaiah about eunuchs: For *thus saith the Lord to the eunuchs: "They that shall keep my sabbaths, and shall choose the things that please me, and shall hold fast my covenant; I will give to them in my house, and within my walls, a place, and a name better than sons and daughters; I will give them an ever-lasting name which shall never perish"* (Isa 56:4-5). "According to Philostratus in his little book *On Athletes*, the centaurs abstained from leaping and their other sport before a race. It would be reprehensible to exert ourselves more sluggishly for the victory prize of eternal life than ordinary men do for a reward of little worth."[45] Let us consider that it was writ-

44. Averbode *molestia*; Valvekens *modestia*. Valvekens here softens Panhausen's misogyny.
45. See Smaragdus, *Summarium in epistolas et evangelia. Epistola ad Cor. I,* c. 9, PL 102:559B.

ten that the eunuchs who castrated themselves for the kingdom of heaven (I believe this signifies virgins) always follow the Lamb wherever he shall go.

47. Let us beg daily of Christ, the highest, greatest one, with constant prayers that he preserve the flower of our modesty undiminished. With our entire heart let us ask God to liberate us from the foul fire of lustful desire. Then Christ surely will make our mind willing that we not be burned by the flame of fornication, as he does for the chaste. We must then most of all avoid other occasions of this sin, especially leisure, the particular seedbed of all evils including fornication and lust. From this source stem all empty pleasures and association with those evil folk who are the wicked audience for this and all manner of baseness. Finally, if you wish to be a stranger to the vice of lust, be careful to avoid the vice of drunkenness. Let excess and too much drinking be absent, for a belly hot with wine easily boils over into lust. Do not therefore indulge in wine to excess, beyond necessity.

48. The opinion of the Apostle is well known. He asserts, *For you know this and understand, that any fornicator or unclean or covetous* (Eph 5:5) person, or one polluted by any other kind of desire, is not admitted to that shared inheritance of immortal life with Christ that God has promised to his own. If this punishment seems light to you, then believe those who attempt to persuade you that these are light sins. But let no one seduce you by inane words of this kind! Even if such vices are not punished here by human laws, nevertheless for these sins divine vengeance will rage against those who, refusing to trust in the promises of God, rest their happiness in vices of this sort. *Mortify therefore your members which are upon the earth; fornication, uncleanness* (Col 3:5), effeminacy, adultery, and other fetid desires that should remain unnamed lest we be deprived of that inheritance that God has promised to those who love him.

49. When Solomon was seized by the desire for worldly things, he considered them great and admirable, and expended much labor and concern upon them. But when he took charge of himself—as if turning from a certain shadowy abyss he could look again on the light of true wisdom—he cried out in a phrase worthy of heaven, *Vanity of vanities, all is vanity* (Eccl 1:1). If you wish this realization or still more, you will lift your concern from the stormy pleasure of the world and separate yourself from evil habits as you are able.

50. But let us make an end to this subject and hasten to the other part of this matter, true poverty, which in the name of Christ we willingly undertake. We will recognize from our threshold our opponents, those well-armed enemies of virtue, namely concupiscence of the eyes, avarice, as fit only to be kept outside, and we will openly resist their detestable evil.

On the Vow of Poverty

51. Poverty of spirit is the root and foundation of the whole of the Gospel, indeed of Christian truth. This poverty cannot be haughty and prideful, but rather is modest. Without doubt poverty pertains most of all to those who, having left behind everything, perfectly follow Christ according to the example of Peter the apostle. As our Savior says, he who *doth not renounce all that he possesses, cannot be my disciple* (Luke 14:33). *And every one that hath left house, or brethren, or sisters, or father, or mother, or lands, because of my name, shall receive an hundred fold, and shall possess life everlasting* (Matt 19:29).

52. If we wish to be disciples of Christ, it is necessary that we remember to follow in his footsteps. To follow Christ is nothing other than to imitate him. As he walked, we should walk in renewal of life, putting aside the baggage of riches to embrace true poverty. For Christ himself was born a pauper from a poor mother; he did not have a bed in the inn,

he was born in a stable, was laid down in a manger. As an adult he chose disciples for himself not from the herd of the wealthy, but instead fishermen from the community of paupers, who left all behind and followed the naked Christ. And although they had left all things behind, nothing was lacking for them. For so holds the evangelical saying: *When I sent you without purse, and scrip, did you want anything?* And they responded, *Nothing, Lord* (Luke 22:35).

53. Christ, although he was Lord of earth and sea, and of all things under heaven, *hath not a place where to lay his head* (Luke 9:58). When a two-drachma piece was needed for payment, neither Christ nor Peter had money in their girdles or purse. But they caught a fish at Christ's command, and they discovered a four-drachma silver coin in its mouth and thus could pay the boatman.[46] And so also it is certain that the remaining apostles were complete strangers to money and the use of temporal things, for when they were called to apostolate (Matt 10), they voluntarily deprived themselves of this sort of burden.

54. Our Savior hung naked on the cross. He was not honored even with a shroud, or with his own tomb where he might be buried. He was given vinegar to drink on the cross. He asked for water from the Samaritan woman—not something special, or wine; he fed the famished crowd with barley loaves; he weakened and afflicted himself by fasting for forty days. And why not? Do you not believe that he suffered all these things for you, so that you also may learn to be content with your daily food and drink, to weaken your body by fasting and reduce it to servitude, so that you may be able to overcome and conquer the enticements of the flesh and temptations of demons? He cultivated poverty so much that he might teach by his own example to condemn

46. See Matt 17:23-26.

earthly things and meditate on celestial ones, not to take delight in fragile things, but rather in those eternal things that last forever. Who thinks it splendid and suitable, I ask, that the slave possesses riches, while the Lord delights and rejoices in the straits[47] of poverty? Who would bear this injury with a calm mind?

55. Therefore let religious vowed to poverty be ashamed, let priests of God consecrated to the sacred altars be ashamed, and in the same manner let all Christians be ashamed, they who have received their salvific name from Christ and profess themselves to be servants of Christ yet glory in the riches of this world, placing their hope there and attending to the desires of the flesh. Let them forever say farewell to mammon and become rich men in Christ. Let them take care to renounce all these things at least in their heart even if they do not all shun this world in body. In doing so they not only become observers of the commandments of God but actually remove from their midst those things standing in the way, such as the burdens of wealth and other things of that sort. For poverty and wealth lie less in the possession of things than in the disposition of feelings. We might end this counsel on the embrace of poverty with a few more words, which leave something to the will of the one taking it up. For so says the Lord: *If thou wilt be perfect, go sell what thou hast and thou shalt have treasure in heaven; and come follow me* (Matt 19:21).

56. Here the Lord not only counsels but even appears to add a spur to make us more willing to embrace his counsel. He mentions the greatness of the reward to entice and console us. For the Lord promises that he who is a pauper because he has left all things behind because of Christ will have treasure in heaven, receive a hundredfold reward, and

---

47. Averbode *angustiis*; Valvekens *augustis*.

possess life eternal. The apostles professed and cultivated poverty of this sort, and in their name Peter boldly spoke: *Behold we left behind all things and have followed thee* (Matt 19:27). Christians of the earliest church followed this practice as they sold their own possessions and gave the profits to a common use, so that no one said anything was his own, since things remained common among them.[48]

57. Therefore let us embrace voluntary poverty in Christ, since treasure in heaven depends on poverty. Let us cast off the burdens of riches, since eternal woe hangs over wealth; he who has them here has his own consolation upon the earth.[49] *He that hath ears to hear, let him hear* (Matt 11:15). We learn from the comments of Saint Paul that concupiscence of the eyes—avarice, diametrically opposed to this excellent poverty—amounts to worship of idols.[50]

58. What point is there in the effort to garner riches when we are suddenly compelled to leave those things to others? For just as we brought none of those things with us when we were born into this world, so dying we will take nothing out of it.[51] But once avarice or zeal for riches infests the minds of some, they invest their concern in lowly matters and fall into the snare of the devil, into many desires not only for foolish things, but also for pernicious and harmful ones. And indeed desire for possession does not come alone, but leads a huge train of evils along with it—pride of life, violence, fraud, injury, luxury, pleasures, and other diseases of their kind—which plunge men down into ruin and perdi-

---

48. See Acts 2:44-46 and *Rule of St Augustine*, 1.3. An interesting marginal note in the manuscript cites "Nicephorus Lib. 2, cap. 2," referring to *Libri XVIII Ecclesiasticae Historiae* of the fourteenth-century Byzantine ecclesiastical historian Nicephorus. See PG 145:754–55.

49. See Luke 6:24.

50. See Eph 5:5.

51. See 1 Tim 6:7.

tion. Whoever has avarice in his mind does everything in an impure and corrupt fashion.

59. Immoderate desire is the root and seedbed of all evils, and those grasping after it have wandered from faith and entangled themselves in many sorrows. They obtain by great troubles what they then guard with anxious solicitude. If it happens that these things are ripped away, their greedy and avaricious heart is gravely wounded.[52] Men hunt worldly things[53] as their reward, but let us seek rather that we grow wealthy in the true goods of the soul, in piety, content with the things at hand that suffice for the necessity of this present life, that is, nourishment and clothing. Let our character be content with present things without avarice, and God will not desert or abandon us.[54] Therefore the Lord paternally admonishes us, saying, *Take heed and beware of all covetousness; for a man's life doth not consist in the abundance of things which he possesseth* (Luke 12:15). Frequently, under the pretext of necessity or providence, a sad vice creeps in and, once admitted, leads a person into every disgrace. It can hardly be avoided unless we master it with detachment and contempt.[55]

60. An abundance of things makes for anxiety about those possessions rather than for happiness, or for striving for those things still sought. Nature's needs are met by just a little. Avarice has no boundaries. Avarice and excessive desire for things not only do not lead one to help a needy neighbor, but even lead to unjustly grasping everything belonging to others. Avarice is content with no abundance; on the contrary, he who has already gathered many things is the more desirous. Hence that opinion of Solomon: They

---

52. See 1 Tim 6.
53. Averbode *mundani;* Valvekens *mundum.*
54. Marginal note cites 1 Tim 6; Heb 13.
55. Averbode *contemptim;* Valvekens *contemptum.*

take away what is not their own (Prov 11:24). And he who gathers more things may expect a more miserable end. Solomon, that master of parables and mysteries, says, *Substance got in haste shall be diminished; but that which by little and little is gathered with the hand, shall increase* (Prov 13:11).

61. We must curse the avarice of certain men[56] who neither abstain from usury nor fear to falsify prices, who deliberately cheat by weight and measure, selling some coins and buying others. It neither bothers nor shames them to benefit from deception and fraud so that they may become rich. Concerning such men David remembered in his own songs, *But vain are the sons of men, the sons of men are liars in the balances, that by vanity they may together deceive* (Ps 61:10). Indeed, human affairs are all empty, but still many place their trust[57] in fleeting matters as if they were lasting. They despise equity, hold the balance scales of the mind unevenly, condemning justice and rejoicing in injustice. Yet from all this they accrue no benefit, because all these rapidly changing things are vain.

62. But you, O sons of men, do not place hope in iniquity, lest you consider happiness gathered from iniquity worthy of your love. Do not lose your mind seeing riches[58] flowing toward your homes like a river. This greedy monster is cruel and pestilential. Unless we keep watch it will consume us wherever it will into its own lumpy mass.[59] *So the ways of every covetous man destroy the souls of the possessors* (Prov 1:19). Nothing is more pernicious than avarice.[60] Therefore the Lord through the prophet cries out, saying, *For the iniquity of his covetousness I was angry, and I struck him* (Isa 57:17). Who

---

56. Valvekens omits *hominum*.
57. Averbode *confidunt*; Valvekens *consulunt*.
58. Averbode *opes*; Valvekens *spes*.
59. Averbode *pertrahat*; Valvekens *protrahat*.
60. See Sir 10:10.

may list the reasons for all this avarice? It compels men to go against men, and from it arise plots and thefts. When we are not content with our own, we lust after the goods of others, and thence come wars and mutual bloodshed. From this arise disagreements among close relatives, lawsuits between close friends, even relations, all for the sake of hastening an inheritance. For that reason a certain poet has sung, *sons inquired into their fathers' years before the time.*[61]

63. This savage, rabid, and insatiable beast—the power and animalistic love of material possession—progresses to such a point that it is never filled by any draught, but always thirsts like Tantalus over the fountain: "To what crime do you not drive the hearts of men, accursed hunger for gold?"[62]

64. You have sought much for yourself. On the same scale, you nevertheless seek more, and more urgently. The divine Solomon raises a famous example when he says, *There is but one, and he hath not a second, no child, no brother, and yet he ceaseth not to labour, neither are his eyes satisfied with riches, neither doth he reflect saying: for whom do I labour, and defend my soul of good things?* (Eccl 4:8). The Lord threatens men of this sort with a curse, saying, *Woe to you that join house to house and lay field to field, even to the end of the place: shall you alone dwell in the midst of the earth?* (Isa 5:8).

65. For who else may dwell on earth alone other than one who desires to possess all things? From the least to the greatest, all follow avarice. But when Christ entered the temple he cast out buyers and sellers,[63] desiring to show that avarice and

61. Ovid, *Metamorphoses* 1.148. For this translation, see Ovid, *Metamorphoses*, trans. Frank Justus Miller (Cambridge, MA: Harvard University Press, 1916), 1:13.

62. Virgil, *Aeneid* 3.56–57. For this translation, see Virgil, *Eclogues. Georgics. Aeneid Books 1–6*, trans. H. Rushton Fairclough (Cambridge, MA: Harvard University Press, 1916), 377.

63. See Luke 19:45.

profit would be deadly diseases for the church that temple prefigured. If in any age this great greed of possession has sunk deeply into human hearts, it does so now most of all. For that reason, let us who have bound ourselves by a vow of poverty adhere to it perpetually, and let us take care to put this beast I call avarice far from us. For what does virtue have in common with vice? Or poverty with avarice?

But let us go on now to the third vow, which is humble obedience. It always wages an internal war with pride—nor does it rest in one place or have a fixed abode. But in all these things as well truth will conquer.

On the Vow of Obedience

66. Obedience and humility are the seedbed[64] of all the other virtues, without which little or nothing else is acceptable before the highest God. Pride of life cruelly opposes itself to this virtue but will achieve nothing by it. *They that trust in the Lord shall be as Mount Sion, he shall not be moved forever* (Ps 124:1). For those who deny themselves display obedience and of their own accord renounce not only their desires but indeed their very wills. In no matter do they desire to be under their own control, but rather under the will of another. They also are not satisfied to live by their own judgment, which they instead give over to Christ, whose will and command they most gladly follow.

67. The church has always had faithful imitators of the excellent Christ, as ancient admirers, namely the historians Philo, Eusebius, and Nicephorus, demonstrate.[65] These esteemed and upright companies of pious and religious men—beyond the habit and example of ordinary folk—left behind all goods and delightful enticements of the flesh, and were

64. Averbode *seminarium*; Valvekens *summarium*.
65. Valvekens omits the names of the philosophers found in Averbode.

zealous for holy obedience according to their religious profession. They arranged their lives completely according to the example of Christ's obedience and to the perfection of the evangelical standard, meditating on the law of the Lord by day and night.[66] In this matter, we have excellent witnesses—Basil, Augustine, Jerome, Benedict, Cassian, and innumerable other teachers of evangelical perfection and most expert observers of the monastic institution.

68. Christ, the most perfect exemplar of evangelical perfection, not only teaches this counsel of obedience in his word, but also commends himself to us by the example of his own life, when he is obedient to the Father *even to the death of the cross* (Phil 2:8). And about himself Christ gave testimony, saying, *I came down from heaven, not to do my own will, but the will of him that sent me* (John 6:38). Truly Christ here means the will of the Father, and of those to whom it is read that he was made subject. Again urging us to imitate his own model, Christ says, *If any man will come after me, let him deny himself, take up his cross, and follow me* (Matt 16:24).

69. "Beyond this, the goal of apostolic preaching and doctrine was obedience of faith in the name of Jesus, so that by obeying the truth, the souls of the faithful might be purified through the Holy Spirit with fraternal charity, which by the grace of God eternal life follows."[67] We read that Christ, so that he might entice us to imitation of this virtue, responded thus to his mother and Joseph: *Did you not know, that I must be about my father's business?* (Luke 2:49). Christ said this very thing, so that we might imitate his example in this very act of obedience. First of all, let us show obedience to God, then to parents—and indeed to the magistracy—with compliance. He himself, as the Evangelist

---

66. See Ps 1:2.
67. See Smaragdus, *Summarium in epistolas et evangelia*, PL 102:554.

witnesses, showed himself compliant to them: *He went down with them . . . and was subject to them* (Luke 2:51).

70. What further? Does not God always exalt the humble and scatter the arrogant with the mind of his own heart?[68] The mind and spirit of the proud are unable to rest and always rouse themselves further. Hence in Obadiah the prophet the Lord severely rebukes Idumea when he says, *The pride of thy heart hath lifted thee up, who dwellest in the clefts of the rocks, and settest up thy throne on high: who sayest in thy heart: who shall bring me down to the ground? Though thou be exalted as an eagle, and though thou sit thy nest among the stars: thence will I bring thee down, saith the Lord* (Obad 1:3-4). Furthermore, the divine accompanist David reminded us: *I have seen the wicked highly exalted, and lifted up like the cedars of Libanus; and I passed by, and lo, he was not; and I sought him and his place was not found* (Ps 36:35-36).

71. That illustrious David saw the end of the kingdom of Saul and the overthrow of Absalon—as well as the arrogant death of the foreigner Goliath—and the final destruction of still more arrogant men than these. Rightly he compared their foulness with sterile trees.[69] Indeed not only did David say that they themselves were vain, but he compared them to places of desolation. Everyone, the Savior says, who humbles himself will be exalted, and who exalts himself will be humbled.[70]

72. Humility and pride are as far from each other as can be. Pride draws its origin from the root of self-love and self-will, and it is the very worst of all evils. The origin of every sin is that pride hateful to God and men. All the more then should you shun this pestilent evil. Let the fall of Lucifer be an example to you, who on account of the vice of pride was

68. See Luke 1:51-52.
69. See Ps 1.
70. See Luke 14:11 and Matt 23:12.

cast down from the sublime dwelling place of the heavens. His imitators seek the height and are puffed up in spirit, so they fear neither God nor men.[71] And although every iniquity is performed in evil deeds so that pride breaks the boundaries of all wickedness, still its cruel attendants[72] are so beset by good works that they are overwhelmed and perish.

Daughters of Pride[73]

73. Among these attendants are excessive self-assurance, appetite for empty glory, contempt of others, and a tendency to vomit forth self-praise, to suffer no one to be superior to oneself, and not even to show good naturedness to equals. Still more are immodest bearing and dress, harsh words, a stiff neck, insolent appearance, and haughty eyes, which the Lord will humble. Fearing this, Jesus the son of Sirach prayed, saying, *O Lord father and God of my life . . . give me not haughtiness of my eyes* (Sir 23:4-5). That is, let not pride overcome me, and do not let me think that I am something above what I really am.

74. *Among the proud there are always contentions* (Prov 13:10), while upon the humble and obedient rests the spirit of the Lord. A proud man suffers himself to be bested by no one; a humble and truly obedient man submits himself to all the laws of charity. A proud man is invested in this, that he diminishes a neighbor by his own false accusations and degrades him as of little worth, but raises himself up. The humble and broken in heart lovingly embraces his neighbor with a fair scale of judgment and in his own eyes is very small. The proud man pours forth the virulence of his soul

---

71. Averbode *verentur*; Valvekens *vocantur*. Valvekens also omits *Deum*.

72. Averbode *pedissiquae*; Valvekens *dissequi*.

73. Averbode *filiae*; Valvekens *filii*.

into others and, when he has sustained an injury, retaliates with punishment.

75. Humble obedience holds all things in common with her sister charity and thus is patient and kind and does not rejoice over wrongdoing, but rather rejoices together with truth. She does not envy, does not act falsely, is not puffed up, and is not ambitious, but endures all things patiently.[74] The Lord says, *The reproaches of them that reproached thee are fallen upon me* (Ps 68:10). I moreover *will keep thy justifications* (Ps 118:8). *They have spoken against me with deceitful tongues; and they have compassed me about with words of hatred; and have fought against me without cause. Instead of making me a return of love, they detracted me: but I gave myself to prayer* (Ps 108:3-4), and in you, Lord, I took refuge, opposed as I was on every side. *But not so the wicked, not so* (Ps 1:4). Indeed, the wicked are neither moved nor left in peace by a kind warning, by the authority of a magistrate, finally not even by the severity of laws. Instead they walk forth according to their own desires, and in every lawful and unlawful thing—the commission of crimes—they believe themselves to be devout. Thus Joab, the leader of David's army, did not accept the honor of his command and could not share in the praises of the army. Instead, after pretending to address his colleague Amasa in a friendly manner, he murdered the unwary man.[75]

76. So pride abstains from no crime, including robbery, nor does it refrain from slaughter. While pride strives to exalt and overcome everyone, it is not at all content to be within its own limits. Confidence in force incites some, while others are excited by wealth of material possessions. Still others in their recklessness over time see the apparent benefit of sinning until they finally by their persistence in

---

74. See 1 Cor 13:4-6.
75. See 2 Sam 20 (Vulg 2 Kgs 20).

crimes and blindness of conscience are restrained neither by shame of men nor by any fear of God. Rightly it is, therefore, that Saint John perceives this serpentine beast among the three evils of the world when he says, *For all that is in the world is the concupiscence of the flesh and the concupiscence of the eyes and the pride of life* (1 John 2:16).

77. When we make the effort to resist vices, there is a reward for us. For to the extent that one hates faults, that deeply does he desire the good of virtues opposed to the worldly realm. So, my dearly beloved, let us shun the execrable evil of pride, leaving it far behind us, and let us adhere to humble obedience, the mother and guardian of all virtues. In holy obedience let us train ourselves throughout all our days, as long as breath is in our limbs.

Summary of the Three Evangelical Counsels

78. Now I will say a bit about the evangelical counsels I mentioned earlier. Doubtless we are inflamed to faith and the exercises of devotion by certain incitements of faith and piety. As we become warm to devotion, spiritual weapons arm us against the world's infirmities and allurements of the flesh, while the efforts of good men support us toward better things. These supports renew the spirit and prepare it better for the fulfillment of religious duty and divine worship, and provide us easy access to those eternal rewards promised to us by God. Finally, we find the height of evangelical perfection in this—that as best we can we swiftly strive toward those virtues that preserve us in both the fear and the love of God. Let us imitate Christ, who as a pauper and virgin was preeminently obedient to the Father through all things unto death, even on the cross.[76]

---

76. See Phil 2:8.

Let us leave behind the desires of the world—luxury, avarice, and pride of life. Let chastity, poverty, and humble
obedience take their place.

79. We must not lack charity, the bond of perfection and
summation of the law. Without it every virtue is imperfect,
and chastity, poverty, obedience—in the end all our acts of
justice—will be as dust, which the wind[77] blows from the
face of the earth. Happy that man whose heart the love of
Christ and charity have wounded with a sharpened spear.
Charity alone offers a living person to God as a victim and
acceptable sacrifice. "This makes true religious, this makes
monks; without this monasteries are hells and those dwelling in them demons. But indeed, if this charity is present,
monasteries are *paradises of pomegranates* (Song 4:13) and
lilies of the valleys (Song 2:1) on the earth, and those living
in them are angels."[78]

80. Therefore, although long fasts waste the body or abject
clothes misshape it, if inner charity is lacking we have not
come to the lowest step of religious life. Indeed, no way of
life is worse for our preferment than to dwell together in
body but not in mind. There ought to be one love,[79] one
will, one pattern of behavior, lest what pleases one displease
the other, or one be glad when another is grieved. If we
direct our[80] life in this manner, our way of living will please
God on high, for he makes those of one character to dwell
in a home, and we will be perfect followers of the primitive
church, in which *a multitude of believers had but one heart and
one soul, and all things were in common unto them* (Acts 4:32).[81]
Through Jeremiah the prophet the Lord announced this

77. Valvekens omits *ventus*.
78. See PsJerome, *Regula monachorum ad Eustochium*, chap. 1, PL 30:393.
79. Averbode *affectus*; Valvekens *effectus*.
80. Valvekens omits *nostram*.
81. See also *Rule of St Augustine*, chap. 1.

thing to come in the future, saying, *And I will give them one heart, and one* soul, *that they may fear me all days; and that it may be well with them, and their children . . . . And I will make an everlasting covenant with them, and will not cease to do them good* (Jer 32:39-40). 81. O holy society! O heavenly congregation of devout men who, made in flesh, live outside the flesh, *meditating on the law of the Lord day and night* (Ps 1:2). I urge you and beg you, my most beloved sons and brothers in Christ—you who have already made profession and are dead and buried with Christ—to guard yourselves as pilgrims and sojourners from the carnal desires that beset the soul. Put all your trust in God, who cares for you. Here know that *no servant can serve two masters: for either he will hate the one, and love the other; or he will hold to the one, and despise the other* (Luke 16:13). If you wish to be a slave to the world and its desires, there is no safety for you in Christ. But if you renounce the world's desires and join yourself to God, your reward is rich in heaven. You cannot serve both God and the world: you must renounce one. *For what participation hath justice with injustice . . . . And what concord hath Christ with Belial?* (2 Cor 6:14, 15). *All whatsoever you do in word or in work, do all in the name of the Lord Jesus Christ* (Col 3:17). *Therefore whether you eat, or drink, or whatsoever else you do, do all toward the glory of God* (1 Cor 10:31), and take care that you walk without offense in the house of God, having one heart and one mind in all things pleasing to God and toward the good.[82] So the Apostle Paul was pleasing in all things—not seeking what would be useful to himself but rather to the many, that they be saved.[83]

---

82. See *Rule of St Augustine*, chap. 1.
83. See 1 Cor 10:33.

82. My dearly beloved brothers, my joy and the crown of my glory, keep watch, stand firm in the faith, act manfully, and be strengthened. Let all that you do be done in charity. For as long as you judge that you yourself are standing firm, then most of all you need watchfulness and wariness lest you fall. He who stands upright must especially beware lest he fall.[84] So stand tall that you may be perfect and full in charity, all wisdom, prudence, and the will of the Lord.

83. To abandon your intention for a more honest life and revert to sensual pleasure is pernicious. From good you will become[85] evil, from just unjust, from an innocent man a sinner. Let me employ the words of Saint Peter: *For it had been better for them not to have known the way of justice, than after they have known it, to turn back from that holy commandment which was delivered to them* (2 Pet 2:21). For the most part, this happens from error or ignorance. But there are those who, once having recognized the way of truth, at first flee from the pollutions of this world and profess a pure and celestial life. Then, overcome by desire, they are wound up again by their old sordid ways. Not only does their previous way of life stir them up, but they are left in even a worse state than they were before they embraced that celestial and pure life. Concerning this pattern, the prophet presents the opinion of the Lord, saying, *But if the just man turn himself away from his justice, and do iniquity according to all the abominations which the wicked man useth to work, shall he live? All his justices which he hath done, shall not be remembered; in the prevarication, by which he hath prevaricated, and in his sin, which he hath committed, in them he shall die* (Ezek 18:24). *And he that passeth over from justice to sin, God hath prepared such an one for the sword* (Sir 26:27) and vengeance.

---

84. Averbode *Qui enim stat, videat non cadat*; Valvekens *Qui enim stare se cadat.*

85. Averbode *fieris*; Valvekens *fueri.*

No one, says the Savior, *putting his hand to the plow, and looking back, is fit for the kingdom of God* (Luke 9:62).

Concerning Pride and the Disease of Avarice[86]

84. Do not think that if you relapse into sin God will spare you just because he is merciful. I do not believe that at all. For if he did not spare Lucifer with his consorts—who led by haughtiness of mind and desired to be like unto God the Most High—neither will he spare you, O earth, dust, and ash! For that man who was the Lord's own accountant and bore the money bag and wallet for him profited nothing when, drunk with the passion of avarice, he sold his most beloved and also merciful Lord to the Jews, handing him over to be crucified and killed. But Judas himself received the recompense of his own action, as he ended his life by strangulation, to be tortured by eternal fire.

85. In the history written in the Book of Numbers is found the notorious fornication of the people of Israel with the daughters of Moab, on account of which twenty-four thousand of the people were killed. Nor did that misfortune cease until Phineas the son of Eleazar drove a spear through the genitals of Zambri and the Madianite prostitute, the man and the woman both, for the same base sin of fornication.[87] From this story we learn how abominable is the sin of lust.

86. Tell me, I beg you, which is more detestable, to walk about naked, or to commit adultery or rape? No one doubts that the latter is worse, and nevertheless no one dares willingly to walk about nude, fearful of shame. But all dare to commit adultery and other illicit sexual acts. They not only dare but even long to do so, and about these things and

---

86. I have combined these two headings, which in the text are separated by two sentences.

87. See Num 25.

about their own entertainments they glory and exult. Surely to fornicate, commit adultery, or calumniate are not at all consistent with being a good man. But the world cultivates these things, along with other wicked activities of this kind. The Apostle inveighs against this: *Know you not that your bodies are the members of Christ? Shall I then take the members of Christ and make them the members of an harlot? God forbid!* (1 Cor 6:15). The Lord will judge fornicators and adulterers, as Paul says in another place: *For know you this and understand: that no fornicator or unclean or covetous person hath inheritance in the kingdom of Christ* (Eph 5:5). Let it not be so. God will judge. And elsewhere we read: know this, you who understand, that no fornicator or impure man will inherit the kingdom of Christ. Do not be seduced: for neither fornicators or adulterers, nor effeminates or men who lie with other men, will possess the kingdom of God. Grave is the sentence, but graver still the punishments.

87. I exhort you in the Lord, most beloved brethren, that when the human mind conceives harmful, pestilent, and lustful thoughts, you take care to obliterate them directly in the seed, lest you let the children of Babylon sprout among you. Do not make friends with those who may work toward your ruin.[88] For they are sons of fornication and not genuine; their mother is an adulteress who has fornicated with many lovers. Put aside such things and choose those that are better. And once you have raised your mind to this high standard of life, remain in it steadfastly, bearing all things with a strong spirit even if they seem too severe and harsh. Bow your necks to the yoke of obedience, preferring to submit to the will of another rather than to follow your own. Cultivate poverty, possessing or even desiring nothing of your own. Let growing rich in virtue be your sole concern. Break the wantonness of the flesh and the dregs of

---

88. See Exod 34:12.

various lusts by fasting; so pruned, a good tree can bring forth good fruits. *Every tree therefore which does not yield good fruit shall be cut down and cast into the fire* (Matt 3:10).

88. All mortal beings must fear this saying, but deadly and pestilential kinds of men who rejoice when they have done evil and exult in the worst things should be especially afraid. If fruitlessness will be thrown into the fire, what may greed anticipate? If the slothful who have brought no benefit to mortal men will burn, what about those who bring condemnation and poverty upon their neighbors through fraud? If they who have not nourished the hungry will be called *cursed* in the final Day of Judgment, for what harshness will those be singled out who are themselves nourished by evil itself, and wickedness? If they who did not clothe the naked will be commanded to proceed into eternal fire, how will they be excepted who have plundered those who have garments?[89] In our own days it is not considered shameful to violate all laws—divine justice and the justice of human society together—and virtually all these ills originate from an excessive[90] admiration of riches.

89. O foolish greed, sharp and violent, which thrusts him who has it down to deepest hell! Those wise ancients seem to me completely worthy of praise who revealed to the rest of us the way of abdication of the world, a path on which no one's footsteps walked before. Let us flee, most beloved, this more than pestilential world, for it is founded in evil with its lusts. Tell me, I ask, what does this world hold that is not harmful? Here the wounds of disease and calumny, there envy; here hatred, desperation, and daily anxieties, there innumerable plots and perpetual evils coming from every direction. As one who sweetens the ears of men with poetry puts it, *You lads, who cull flowers*

---

89. See Matt 25:41-43.
90. Averbode *immodica*; Valvekens *omnimoda*.

and strawberries that grow so low, be gone from here; a chill snake lurks in the grass.[91]

90. Let us flee the world, let us go with Christ into a desert place, and let us follow John the Baptist and others who sought the desert not only in the body but even in mind. Let us flee the wiles of the ancient serpent. Let us restrain a lying tongue from evil just as if it were a stumbling foot, and let our lips not speak deception and iniquity. Let hatred be gone, envy absent, pain and discord banished afar. Finally, let us call back the mind from all semblance of evil, and, doing only good, let us seek after peace and pursue it.[92] This is the height of all good things. *For the eyes of the Lord are directed upon the just, and his ears unto their prayers. But, the countenance of the Lord is against them that do evil things, to cut off the remembrance of them from the earth* (Ps 33:15-16).

91. God requires first from devout men that they cultivate gentleness and mildness and, as much in themselves as toward others, to be zealous for peace. So with the greatest diligence we must search out the path and way of thinking how we ourselves may lay hold of this most sweet fruit of devotion, an incomparable treasure. Then with no less zeal we must strive to reach, that is, to pursue peace—and then maintain it.

92. But when we examine all things with thought and mind, we discover that there is really one method to obtain this divine good. And that is to despise riches, honor, life, and all things human, and devoutly and in a holy manner dedicate ourselves in servitude to God. Content under his protection, we can let the rest go easily, with a glad heart. Then without doubt the eye of the Lord will be upon us and, when we seek[93] good things from God, our prayers

---

91. Virgil, *Eclogues* 3.92. For this translation, see Virgil, *Eclogues*, trans. Fairclough, 47.

92. See Ps 33:14.

93. Averbode *quaesiverimus*; Valvekens *fecerimus*.

will obtain them. On the other hand, God indeed will recognize those who can have peace neither with God nor with their neighbor, nor even with their very selves. With his countenance turned in anger—that is, with severe expression—he will pronounce the sentence of death upon them, and so destroy and entirely eradicate their memory from the land of the living. For the most part, the word *face* [*facies*] is understood in Sacred Scriptures to be used for the countenance of God directed toward what is good, but the word *countenance* [*vultus*] when directed toward evil.

93. Let us therefore cultivate peace. As strangers to all passing things, let us cultivate Christian poverty, for poverty herself is the nurse and seedbed of peace. And let us cultivate obedience in Christ without pretense of heart. Let us be ornamented with chastity as men unstained by the pollution of women. For those are virgins who follow the Lamb wherever he goes. If our whole mind rests on these things, neither concupiscence of the flesh or eyes nor pride of life may hold us as its own. But now we are weary, so let us draw to a close.

94. I beg you, my Lord God, Creator and Redeemer, most graciously to have mercy upon this sinner. May your mercy support me all the days of my life so that finally I may dwell in the house of the Lord as long as I live, and that you may deign by your loving care to lead this vessel tested by every disturbance to a tranquil port, where it may fear no shipwreck or any dejection of sorrow or pain. To you be glory, honor, and power, together with your only begotten Son and the Holy Spirit, for ever and ever. Amen.

The end.

(This copy completed on the feast of the Beheading of John the Baptist, August 29, 1575, by Brother Hermann of Noerwich).

Bibliography

Manuscripts

Averbode. Abdijarchief. IV, hs. 330.

Trier. Stadtbibliothek. hs. 2199/1818.

Editions of Jacob Panhausen's Works

Exhortatio Pia

Valvekens, Jean-Baptiste, ed. "Exhortatio pia abbatis Panhausen, abbatis Steinfeldensis 1572." *Analecta Praemonstratensia* 54 (1978): 166–90.

Praefatio in Regulam Divi Aurelii Augustini Hypponensis Episcopi

Hyland, William P., ed. "Abbot Jacob Panhausen of Steinfeld's *Praefatio in Regulam Divi Aurelii Augustini Hypponensis Episcopi* (1570 Text and Commentary)." *Analecta Praemonstratensia* 94 (2018): 132–59.

Tractatus de Monasticae Vitae Cultoribus atque Religiosorum Votis

Valvekens, Jean-Baptiste, ed. "Abbatis Panhausen Tractatus de Monasticae Vitae Cultoribus atque religiosorum votis." *Analecta Praemonstratensia* 54 (1978): 191–219.

Editions and Translations of Ancient, Patristic, Medieval, and Contemporary Sources[1]

Adam of Dryburgh. *Liber de ordine habitu et professione canonicorum ordinis praemonstratensis* [On the Order, Habit, and Religious Profession of Regular Canons of Premontre]. PL 198:439–610.

---

1. Editions in Patrologiae Latinae cursus completus, and Patrologiae Graecae cursus completus, ed. Jacques-Paul Migne (Paris, 1841–1864), are listed as PL and PG, respectively, with column numbers.

Ambrose. *De Joseph Patriarcha*. PL 14:641–73.

———. *Epistle 42*. PL 16:1123–29.

Anselm of Havelberg. *Epistola apologetica,* PL 188:1091–1118. Trans. Theodore J. Antry and Carol Neel. *Norbert and Early Norbertine Spirituality*. New York: Paulist Press, 2007. 29–62.

Aquinas, Thomas. *Summa Theologiae: Summa Theologica of St Thomas Aquinas*. Trans. Fathers of the English Dominican Province. New York: Benzinger Brothers, Inc., 1948. Reprinted by Christian Classics, 1981.

Augustine of Hippo. *Confessions*. Trans. Henry Chadwick. Oxford: Oxford University Press, 1991.

———. *Homily 2 on I John*. Trans. H. Browne. Nicene and Post-Nicene Fathers, First Series, 7. Ed. Philip Schaff. Buffalo, NY: Christian Literature Publishing Co., 1888.

———. *Règle de saint Augustin* [Rule of Saint Augustine]. Ed. Luc Verheijen. 2 vols. Paris: Études Augustiniennes, 1967.

Benedict of Nursia. *RB 1980: Rule of St Benedict*. Ed. and trans. Timothy Fry. Collegeville, MN: Liturgical Press, 1981.

Bernard of Clairvaux. *On the Song of Songs II*. Trans. Kilian Walsh. Cistercian Fathers 7. Kalamazoo, MI: Cistercian Publications, 1983.

Biel, Gabriel. *Collectorium sive epitome in magistri sententiarum libros*. Ed. Wilfridus Werbeck and Udo Hofmann. Tübingen: Mohr and Siebeck, 1977.

Bonaventure, *Defense of the Mendicants*. Ed. and trans. Jose de Vinck and Robert J. Karris. St. Bonaventure, NY: Franciscan Institute Publications, 2010.

———. *Disputed questions on Evangelical Perfection*. Ed. and trans. Thomas Reist and Robert J. Karris. St. Bonaventure, NY: Franciscan Institute Publications, 2008.

Calvin, John. *Christianae religionis institutio (editio postrema, 1559)*. Turnhout: Brepols Publishers, 2010.

Campegius, Thomas. *De coelibatu sacerdotu non abrogando*. Venice: Ad signum spei, 1554.

Canones Concilii Provincialis Coloniensis anno celebrati M.D. XXXVI, etc. Paris: apud Audeonum Paruum, 1547.

Erasmus, Desiderius. *Adagia*. Basel: Joa. Frobenius, 1523.

———. *Apothegmatum Libri I–IV*. Ed. Tineke L. Ter Meer. Leiderdorp: E. J. Brill, 2010.

———. *In Laurentii Vallae Elegantiarum libros Epitome*. Cologne: Ioannes Gymnicus, 1542.

———. *Novum Testamentum omne, multo quam antehac diligentius ab Erasmo Roterodamo recognitum, emendatum ac translatum*. Basel: Joa. Frobenius, 1519.

———. *Paraphrasim D. Erasmi Roterodami in Omnes Epistolas Apostolicas, etc*. Basel: Joa. Frobenius, 1532.

———. *Paraphrasis in Evangelium secundum Ioannem*. Basel: Ioa. Frobenius, 1524.

Gellius, Aulus. *Noctes Atticae*. Trans. J. C. Rolfe. Cambridge, MA: Harvard University Press, 2014.

Grotius, Hugo. *Dicta Poetarum quae apud Ioannem Stobaeum exstant*. Paris: Nicolaus Buon, 1626.

Horace. *Satires, Epistles, The Art of Poetry*. Trans. H. Rushton Fairclough. Cambridge, MA: Harvard University Press, 2015.

Iamblichus. *On the Pythagorean Way of Life*. Trans. John Dillon and Jackson Hershbell. Atlanta: Scholars Press, 1991.

Jerome. *Epistola 7 ad Chromatium, Jovinum, et Eusebium*. PL 22:338–41.

John of Landsberg. *A Letter from Jesus Christ to the Soul that really Loves him*. Trans. and ed. John Griffiths. New York: The Crossroad Publishing Company, 1981.

Klingius, Conradus. *Loci Communes Theologici Pro Ecclesia Catholica*. Cologne: Arnoldus Birkmannus, 1559.

Luther, Martin. *An Answer to Several Questions on Monastic Vows*. In Luther's Works, vol. 46. The Christian in Society III. Ed. Robert C. Schulz. Philadelphia: Fortress Press, 1967.

———. *The Judgment of Martin Luther on Monastic Vows*. In Luther's Works, vol. 44. The Christian in Society I. Ed. James Atkinson. Philadelphia: Fortress Press, 1966.

Martial. *Epigrams, Volume II: Books 6–10*. Ed. and trans. D. R. Shackleton Bailey. Cambridge, MA: Harvard University Press, 1993.

Nicephorus. *Libri XVIII Ecclesiasticae Historiae*. PG 145.

Nicholas of Cusa. *Nicholas of Cusa's Didactic Sermons: A Selection*. Trans. Jasper Hopkins. Loveland, CO: The Arthur J. Banning Press, 2008.

Origen. *Homilies on Numbers.* PG 12.

Ovid. *Metamorphoses.* Trans. Frank Justus Miller. Cambridge, MA: Harvard University Press, 2014.

Plutarch. *Moralia: De Placitis Philosophorum.* Trans. Gulielmus Beda. Basel: Ioannis Heruagius, 1531.

———. *Moralia,* vol 3. Trans. Frank Cole Babbitt. 16 vols. Cambridge, MA: Harvard University Press, 1957.

———. *Moralia,* vol. 6. Trans. W. C. Helmbold. 16 vols. Cambridge, MA: Harvard University Press, 1939.

PsAugustine. *Sermones ad fratres in eremo. Sermo V, De Obedientia, ad Sacerdotes Suos.* PL 40:1242–46.

PsBede. *Sermo 18 De Sanctis. Homily 70.* Among Bede's works in PL 94:450B–52C.

PsJerome. *Regula Monachorum, ad Eustochium.* PL 30:391–434.

Reu, J. M., ed. *The Augsburg Confession: A Collection of Sources.* Fort Wayne, IN: Concordia Theological Seminary Press, [n.d.].

Sider, Robert Dick, ed. *New Testament Scholarship: Paraphrases on Romans and Galatians.* Collected Works of Erasmus, vol. 42. Toronto: University of Toronto Press, 1984.

———. *New Testament Scholarship: Paraphrases on Timothy, Titus, Philemon, Peter, James, Jude, John, Hebrews.* Collected Works of Erasmus, vol. 44. Toronto: University of Toronto Press, 1993.

Smaragdus. *Summarium in epistolas et evangelia.* PL 102.

Tanner, Norman, ed. *Decrees of the Ecumenical Councils.* London: Sheed & Ward; Washington, DC: Georgetown University Press, 1990.

Tappert, Theodore, ed. and trans. *The Book of Concord: The Confessions of the Evangelical Lutheran Church.* Philadelphia: Fortress Press, 1959.

Terence. *The Woman of Andros. The Self-Tormentor. The Eunuch.* Trans. John Barsby. Cambridge, MA: Harvard University Press, 2001.

Virgil. *Eclogues. Georgics. Aeneid Books 1–6.* Trans. H. Rushton Fairclough. Cambridge, MA: Harvard University Press, 1916.

Secondary Works

Ahuis, Ferdinand. "Johannes Boldewan." In *Auf den zweiten Blick: Frauen und Männer der Nordkirche vom Mittelalter bis zur Gegen-*

wart. Schriften des Vereins für Schleswig-Holsteinische Kirchengeschichte. Ed. Claudia Tietz, Ruth Albrecht, and Rainer Hering. Husum, Germany: Mathiesen, 2018. 61:61–69.

Ardura, Bernard. "Les exhortations capitulaires de Nicolas Psaume." *Analecta Praemonstratensia* 53 (1987): 26–69.

————. *The Order of Prémontré: History and Spirituality*. Trans. Edward Hagman. De Pere, WI: Paisa Publishing, 1995.

Becchi, Francesco. "Le traduzioni latine dei *Moralia* di Plutarco tra XIII e XVI secolo." In *Plutarco nelle traduzioni latine di età umanistica (Seminario di studi, Fisciano, 12–13 Iuglio 2007)*, edited by Paola Volpe Cacciatore. Naples: Strumenti per la ricerca plutarchea, 2009. 11–33.

Beck, Mark, ed. *A Companion to Plutarch*. Chichester: Wiley Blackwell, 2014.

Bose, Mishtooni. "The Opponents of John Wyclif." In *A Companion to John Wyclif*, edited by Ian Christian Levy. Leiden: E. J. Brill, 2006. 407–55.

Bynum, Caroline Walker. "The Spirituality of Regular Canons in the Twelfth Century." In *Jesus as Mother: Studies in the Spirituality of the High Middle Ages*. Berkeley: University of California Press, 1982. 22–58.

Castelli, Patrizia. "*Lux Italiae*: Ambrogio Traversari Monaco Camaldolese: Idee e Immagini nel Quattrocento Fiorentino." *Atti e memorie dell'Accademia Toscana de scienze e lettere: La Columbaria* 47 (1982): 39–90.

Chaix, Gérald. "La Reception du Chartreux Lansperge Survivance ou Metamorphose de la Devotio Moderna." In *Historia et Spiritualitas Cartusiensis: Acta Colloquii Quarti Internationalis*, edited by Jan De Grawe. Saint-Etienne: Centre Européen de Recherches sur les Congrégations et Ordres Monastiques, 1983. 59–68.

————. *Reforme et Contre-Reforme Catholiques: Recherche sur la Chartreuse de Cologne au XVIe Siecle*. Analecta Cartusiana 80. Salzburg: Institut für Anglistik und Amerikanistik, 1981.

Dodds, Madeleine Hope, and Ruth Dodds. *The Pilgrimage of Grace 1536–1537 and the Exeter Conspiracy 1538*. Cambridge: Cambridge University Press, 1971.

Ells, Hastings. *Martin Bucer*. New Haven: Yale University Press, 1931.

Epp, George K. "The Spiritual Roots of Menno Simons." In *Mennonite Images,* edited by Harry Loewen. Winnipeg: Hyperion Press, 1980. 51–59.

Franzen, August. *Bischof und Reformation: Erzbischof Herman von Wied in Köln von der Entscheidung zwischen Reform und Reformation.* Munster: Aschendorff, 1971.

Frymire, John M. *The Primacy of the Postils: Catholics, Protestants and the Dissemination of Ideas in Early Modern Germany.* Leiden & Boston: E. J. Brill, 2010.

Gerits, Trudo J. "Documents inédite sur les visites canoniques de Jean Despreuts, abbe-general de premontre au XVIe siècle." *Analecta Praemonstratensia* 44 (1968): 117–27.

———. "Jacob Panhuysen van Opoeteren, abt van Steinfeld: Een kloosterhervormer, ascetisch schrijver en humanist uit de 16de eeuw." *Heemkunde Limburg* 2 (2006): 10–15.

Goovaerts, L. *Ecrivains, artistes et savants de l'Ordre de Prémontré.* Brussels: Schepens, 1902–1907.

Grendler, Paul. "The Survival of Erasmus in Italy." *Erasmus in English* 8 (1976): 2–22.

Greschat, Martin. *Martin Bucer: A Reformer and his Times.* Louisville and London: Westminster John Knox Press, 2004.

Greven, Joseph. *Die Kölner Kartause und die Anfänge der Katholischen Reform in Deutschland.* Münster in Westfalen: Aschendorffsche Verlagsbuchhandlung, 1935.

Gribbin, Joseph. *The Premonstratensian Order in Late Medieval Britain.* Woodbridge, UK: Boydell Press, 2001.

Harmless, William. *Mystics.* New York: Oxford University Press, 2008.

Haude, Sigrun. *In the Shadow of "Savage Wolves": Anabaptist Münster and the German Reformation during the 1530s.* Boston: Humanities Press / E. J. Brill, 2000.

———. "The Silent Monks Speak Up: The Changing Identity of the Carthusians in the Fifteenth and Sixteenth Centuries." *Archiv für Reformationgeschichte* 86 (1995): 124–40.

Hyland, William P. "The Climacteric of Late Medieval Camaldolese Spirituality: Ambrogio Traversari, John-Jerome of Prague, and the *Linea Salutis Heremitarum.*" In *Florence and Beyond:*

Culture, Society and Politics in Renaissance Italy, edited by David S. Peterson with Daniel E. Bornstein. Toronto: Centre for Reformation and Renaissance Studies, 2008. 107–20.

———. "Premonstratensian Voices of Reform at the Fifteenth Century Councils." In *Reassessing Reform: A Historical Investigation into Church Renewal*, edited by Christopher M. Bellitto and David Zachariah Flanagin. Washington, DC: Catholic University of America Press, 2012. 208–30.

———. "The Stained Glass *Biblia Pauperum* Windows of Steinfeld Abbey: Monastic Spirituality, Salvation History and the Theological Imagination." In *The Moving Text: David Brown and Biblical Studies in Dialogue*, edited by Christopher R. Brewer, Garrick V. Allen, and Dennis F. Kinlaw III. London: SCM Press, 2018. 143–60.

Kentenich, Gottfried. *Beschreibendes Verzeichnis der Handschriften der Stadbibliothek zu Trier*. Sechtes Heft. Ascetische Schriften. 2. Abteilung. Nachträge. Trier: Kommissionsverlag der Fr. Lintzchen Buchandlung, 1910.

Kirby, David. *Northern Europe in the Early Modern Period: The Baltic World 1492–1772*. London & New York: Longman, 1990.

Klaiber, Wilbirgis, ed. *Katholische Kontroverstheologen und Reformer des 16. Jahrhunderts: ein Werkzeichnis*. Münster in Westfalen: Aschendorffsche Verlagsbuchhandlung, 1978.

Knowles, David. *Bare Ruined Choirs: The Dissolution of the English Monasteries*. Cambridge: Cambridge University Press, 1976.

Leclercq, Jean. Introduction. In *Bernard of Clairvaux: Treatises I*. Cistercian Fathers series 1. Shannon, Ireland: Cistercian Publications, 1970. 15–26.

———. *The Love of Learning and the Desire for God*. Trans. Catharine Misrahi. New York: Fordham University Press, 1982.

Leder, Hans-Günter. *Johannes Bugenhagen Pomeranus—vom Reformer zum Reformator. Studien zur Biographie*. Frankfurt-am-Main: Peter Lang, 2002.

Levy, Ian Christopher. "Wyclif and the Christian Life." In *A Companion to John Wyclif*, edited by Ian Christian Levy. Leiden: E. J. Brill, 2006. 293–364.

Louthan, Howard. *The Quest for Compromise: Peacemakers in Counter-Reformation Vienna*. Cambridge; New York: Cambridge University Press, 1997.

Lugioyo, Brian. *Martin Bucer's Doctrine of Justification: Reformation Theology and Early Modern Irenicism*. Oxford: Oxford University Press, 2010.

Meier, Johannes. "Die nordwestdeutschen Pramonstratenser angesichts von Verfall und Reform des Ordens 1350–1550." *Analecta Praemonstratensia* 79 (2003): 25–56.

Mitchell, Alexander Ferrer. "Preface." In *The Catechism set forth by Archbishop Hamilton, printed at St Andrews 1551*. Edinburgh: W. Paterson, 1892.

Mynors, R. A. B. "The Publication of the Latin Paraphrases." In *New Testament Scholarship: Paraphrases on Romans and Galatians*. Collected Works of Erasmus, vol. 42. Ed. Robert Dick Sider. Toronto: University of Toronto Press, 1984. xi–xix.

Oberman, Heiko. "Martin Luther contra Medieval Monasticism: A Friar in the Lion's Den." In *Ad fontes Lutheri: Toward the Recovery of the Real Luther: Essays in Honor of Kenneth Hagen's Sixty-Fifth Birthday*, edited by Timothy Maschke, Franz Posset, and Joan Skocir. Milwaukee: Marquette University Press, 2001. 183–213.

Oszvald, A. "Fegyverneky Ferenc, sági prépsot, rendi visitator. 1506–1535." In *Emlékkönyu Szent Norbert halálának 800 éves jubileumára*. Gödöll: Jászó-Premontrei Kanonkren, 1934. 51–108.

Pade, Marianne. *The Reception of Plutarch's Lives in Fifteenth-Century Italy*. 2 vols. Copenhagen: Museum Tusculanum Press, 2007.

Paulus, Nikolaus. "Conrad Kling, ein Erfurter Domprediger des 16. Jahrhunderts." *Der Katholik* 74 (1894): 146–63.

Payne, John B., Albert Rabil, Jr., and Warren S. Smith. "The Paraphrases of Erasmus: Origin and Character." In *New Testament Scholarship: Paraphrases on Romans and Galatians*. Collected Works of Erasmus, vol. 42. Ed. Robert Dick Sider. Toronto: University of Toronto Press, 1984. xx–xxix.

Petit, François. *The Norbertine Order: A Short History*. Trans. and ed. Benjamin Mackin, O.Praem. De Pere: St. Norbert Abbey Press, 1963.

———. *Spirituality and History of the Premonstratensians*. Trans. Victor Szczurek. Edited with a foreword by Carol Neel. Cistercian Studies series 242; Premonstratensian Texts and Studies Series 2. Collegeville, MN: Cistercian Publications, 2011.

Pollit, Jacques. *Julius Pflug (1499–1564) et la crise religieuse dans l'Allemagne du XVIe siècle*. Leiden: E. J. Brill, 1990.

Posset, Franz. *The Front-Runner of the Catholic Reformation: The Life and Works of Johann von Staupitz*. Burlington, VT: Ashgate, 2003.

———. *Renaissance Monks: Monastic Humanism in Six Biographical Sketches*. Leiden: E. J. Brill, 2005.

Post, R. R. *The Modern Devotion: Confrontation with Reformation and Humanism*. Leiden: E. J. Brill, 1968.

Pulsfort, Ernst. "Klinge, Konrad," *Biographisch-Bibliographisches Kirchenlexicon* Band 4 (1992): 60–61.

Rummel, Erika. " 'Monachatus non est Pietas': Interpretations and Misinterpretations of a Dictum." In *Erasmus' Vision of the Church*. Sixteenth Century Essays & Studies, vol. XXXII. Ed. Hilmar M. Pabel. Kirksville, MO: Sixteenth Century Journal Publishers, Inc., 1995. 41–56.

Schäfke, Werner, ed. *Die Kölner Kartause um 1500*. Cologne: Kölnisches Stadtmuseum, 1991.

Scribner, R. W. "Civic Unity and the Reformation in Erfurt." *Past and Present* 66 (1975): 29–60.

Selvaggio, Giulio Lorenzo. *Antiquitatum Christianarum Institutiones*. Madrid: Antonio de Sancha, 1779.

Sider, Robert Dick, ed. *New Testament Scholarship: Paraphrases on Timothy, Titus, Philemon, Peter, James, Jude, John, Hebrews*. Collected Works of Erasmus, vol. 44. Toronto: University of Toronto Press, 1993.

Singer, Bruno. *Die Fürstenspiegel in Deutschland im Zeitalter des Humanismus und der Reformation: Biblographische Grundlagen und ausgewählte Interpretationen*. Munich: Wilhelm Fink Verlag, 1981.

Somigli, Costanzo, and Tommaso Bargellini. *Ambrogio Traversari, Monaco Camaldolese: La Figura e la Dottrina Monastica*. Camaldoli: Edizioni Camaldoli, 1986.

Stinger, Charles. *Humanism and the Church Fathers: Ambrogio Traversari (1386–1439) and Christian Antiquity in the Italian Renaissance.* Albany: SUNY Press, 1977.

Stump, Philip H. *The Reforms of the Council of Constance (1414–1418).* Leiden: E. J. Brill, 1994.

Treloar, A. "The Augustinian *Sermones ad fratres in eremo commorantes.*" *Prudentia* 3 (1971): 39–50.

Trippen, Norbert. *Geschichte des Erzbistums Köln.* Cologne: Bachem, 2008.

Valvekens, Jean-Baptiste. "Abbatis I. Panhausen Commentaria in 'Regulam' S. Augustini." *Analecta Praemonstratensia* 54 (1978): 144–65.

———. "Jacobus Panhausen, Abbas Steinfeldensis." *Analecta Praemonstratensia* 54 (1978): 99–104.

———. "Le Chapitre général et les Statuts prémontrés de 1505." *Analecta Praemonstratensia* 13 (1938): 5–46.

Van Spilbeeck, I. *S. Adrien et S. Jacques, de l'Ordre de Prémontré. Martyrs de Gorcum. Notices historiques.* Brussels-Tamine: Bibliothèque Norbertine, 1900.

Vogt, Karl August T. *Johannes Bugenhagen Pomeranus: Leben und ausgewählte Schriften.* Elberfeldt: Verlag von R. L. Friderichs, 1867.

Vos, Lambert (Henri). *Louis de Blois, Abbé de Liesses (1506–1566): Recherches Bibliographiques sur son Oeuvre.* Turnhout: Brepols, 1992.

Zumkellner, Adolar. *Augustine's Ideal of the Religious Life.* New York: Fordham University Press, 1986.

———. *Erbsünde, Gnade, Rechtfertigung und Verdienst nach der Lehre der Erfurter Augustinertheologen des Spätmittelalter.* Cassiciacum 35. Würzburg: Augustinus-Verlag, 1984.

Index of Scriptural References

Scriptural references are identified by page number and, when appropriate, note number.

14:11	15, 78 n. 70
14:33	69
14:26	57
16:2	28
16:13	83
16:19-31	20 n. 29
18:29-30	57
19:45	75 n. 63
21:37	46–47
22:35	70

John

1:29	60
5:41	37
5:44	38 n. 49
6:38	77
14:6	36
17:12	45 n. 7

Acts

2:44-46	72 n. 48
4:12	60
4:32	82
5:1-11	18 n. 21
8:20	18
23:5	21

Romans

	xxxvi, 22 n. 31, 23 nn. 32 and 33
4:8	5
6:16	xlviii, 59
6:18	xlviii, 59
13	xxxiv
13:1-2	22
13:5-6	22

1 Corinthians

2:9	4–5
3:7	56
4:1-2	11
6:15	86
7:25-26	64

7:29	66
7:31	66
7:32-33	64
7:37	66
7:38	66
10:7	13
10:13	63
10:31	83
10:33	83 n. 83
13:4-6	80 n. 74
15:10	63

2 Corinthians

1:12	41
6:14	83
6:15	83
9:7	51
10:3-4	51

Ephesians

4:29	31
5:5	16, 68, 72 n. 50, 86
6:12	51–52
6:13	51

Philippians

1:6	63 n. 40
2:8	77, 81 n. 76
2:13	63, 63 n. 40
3:9	60
4:13	63 n. 39

Colossians

3:5	68
3:17	83
4:5	61

1 Thessalonians

5:8	51

2 Thessalonians

2:3	45 n. 7

Index of Names

Names are cited by page and note number. Scholars are listed separately at the bottom of this index, with page references but without note numbers.

Index of Places

Place names are cited by page number and, when appropriate, note. Place-related references appear at the end of this index.

References Related to Places